Fairytale Christianity

LIVING AS A CHRISTIAN IN THE REAL WORLD

John (JD) Zumwalt

iUniverse, Inc.

New York   Bloomington

iUniverse books may be ordered through booksellers or by contacting:

iUniverse
1663 Liberty Drive
Bloomington, IN 47403
www.iuniverse.com
1-800-Authors (1-800-288-4677)

ISBN: 978-1-4401-7528-2 (pbk)
ISBN: 978-1-4401-7527-5 (ebk)

Printed in the United States of America

iUniverse rev. date: 9/22/2009

In memory of one of the best men I have ever known –
Pastor Ken Hankins.

There is no possibility you knew how many
lives you touched.

I am so sorry I did not tell you so.

Forward

Some folks have an attitude I have come to refer to as *Fairy Tale Christianity*. These are good people who would have you believe that once you become a Christian all your worldly cares will disappear. They try to convince you that you will have no financial problems, you'll never be upset with your spouse, your children will be perfect and you won't get sick. This is just one example of the fact that - as Christians who are attempting to put out the Word of God, we are very often our own worst enemy. This book is an attempt to explain the Christian life, what it means, how we should live it and to point out some of the mistakes that we make along the way. As the reader, your job is to insure that what you are reading in this book is indeed scriptural,[1] otherwise it means nothing. That means that no matter what I say here – you have an obligation to check it out with the Bible.

I also made an attempt to discuss some of the things that we are faced with as Christians. Is the Bible really true in spite of some of the seeming contradictions? Is it a good thing to follow every rule, no matter what? These and a few other questions are discussed in order to attempt to help in our task of living the Christian life.

---

[1]   1st Thessalonians 5:21

Chapter One

I'm a Christian – (So What?)

When you accept Jesus Christ as your Savior (and by the way – what the heck does than even mean? We will discuss that in a bit), it is a huge step. Even if it means nothing else, it means that you are now on your way to heaven. It means you have escaped the horrors of an eternity away from God. If there were no other reason to accept the free gift of salvation – escaping hell would be enough. The truth of the matter though is that there **are** other benefits to Christianity, and that is the very first thing we are going to discuss.

PARACHUTES

When I joined the Army, I wanted to jump out of airplanes. In order to do this I had to go to Army jump school. Jump school is three weeks long. Week one is called *ground week*. Most of that week is spent running, doing chin ups, push ups and being harassed. Most folks that quit, quit in the first week. There are certain things that the Army hammers into you starting with that first week. One of them is the fact that the parachute **will** open. The Jumpmaster repeats that phrase to the students over and over. He wants them to have enough faith in the parachute so that when the time comes for them to jump – they will jump.

The second week of jump school is called *tower week*. During *tower week* we jumped out of towers and slid down a long zip line cable that we were hooked to. It was kind of fun, and all during *tower week* the instructors kept reassuring us that our parachutes were state of the art, and that when we finally did jump from a plane, the parachute <u>would</u> open.

The third week was *jump week*. Every student was looking forward to finally getting to jump out of an airplane. We got our 'chutes on and boarded the plane. That was when I started getting afraid. I seriously began to ask myself what in the world I had been thinking when I signed up. I thought I was afraid when the plane took off, but it turns out I did not yet know what afraid meant. When the jumpmaster opened the door of that airplane, I was trying my best to figure out a way to explain to them that there had been a horrible mistake, and that I was supposed to be in clerk school.

When it came time to actually step out the door I was number seven in line to jump. I'll never forget walking forward towards the door (very quickly) and seeing the heads in front of me disappear - one at a time. All of a sudden all of them were gone and it was my turn. I stepped out the door, gave a couple of terrified grunts, and lo and behold – the parachute opened…just like the jumpmaster said that it would.

Over the years I made lots of jumps. As time went on I learned that I could trust that parachute. I did not have to rely on what someone else told me; I had my own experience to rely on. As my experience grew, so did my faith in the equipment. As time went on and I had several hundred jumps, the fear was replaced by the knowledge that I was going to be OK on these jumps, and that I needed to concentrate on the principles of jumping if I wanted to survive without injury.

I violated those principles early on in jumping. I had just gotten to the 1st Ranger Battalion as a Private First Class. I was participating in my first (real) night jump. The Jumpmaster advised us that it was dark, and that we would not be able to see the ground. He said that since we could not judge our altitude we should remain in our landing position all of the time. (Landing position consists of feet and knees together, toes pointed, legs slightly bent, etc.) Since I am a Zumwalt I figured that I knew more than the jumpmaster - with all of his experience. I paid for thinking that way, as a matter of fact, I still do.

I was about 120 feet in the air (or so I thought), when I hit the ground. Since I thought that I was still 120 feet up, I hit the ground without being in the correct landing position. As a result I sprained my ankle really bad. It swelled up, and turned black on both sides. That injury occurred because I thought I knew more than the Jumpmaster and did not do what he said to do. I did not follow the principles of jumping.

As I jumped over the years I hit hard lots of times. It is not at all unusual for a rucksack in Special Forces to weigh over a hundred pounds. Many times the lightest rucksack on a team will be around 110 pounds. By the time you load ammunition, radios, batteries, food, water, and weapons, a rucksack can easily weigh 130 pounds. As a result, when you jump from the plane you come down very fast. Sometimes you hit harder than others. Sometimes it is because the air is thin in the mountains, or the wind is blowing so hard. Sometimes you don't know why; you just hit hard.

I've had several times when I've hit so hard that I had to lay there a minute to take stock and see if I was OK. In fact, it has taken a minute or two to stop seeing stars. No matter how hard I hit, I was never once tempted to say, *"Man, that is the last time I use a parachute when I jump"*. I always knew that no matter how hard I hit, thank God I had a parachute.

By now you're probably asking what in the world this has to do with salvation. Since I'm getting tired of typing I am really hoping I can tie this together. When we first consider the possibility of becoming a Christian we (normally) don't have a whole lot of faith. How could we? We have no experience. All we know is that someone has told us about their experience and assured us that "the 'chute will open". That gave us just enough faith to step through that door of Christianity. After being Christians for a while we get our own experience and begin to realize that the parachute will open every single time we need it. We begin to develop a faith that is based on our own experience.

Sometimes we get hurt because we start to rely on what we know instead of what God teaches, through His Word. We decide that rather than do what God has told us to do in His instructions, we'll just look around and make our own decisions – because we know more than the "Jumpmaster". Sometimes that attitude causes our twisted ankles.

The longer we live the more weight we carry that makes it easy to get hurt. We have spouses, bills, children, age, etc. As a result of this added weight, sometimes we hit hard – real hard. Some folks in the church I attend have been through some horrendous times. Some are going through hard times right now. I've heard their testimonies and I've seen their pain. I've never heard one of them say, *"Man, that is the last time I wear the parachute of God's love when I go through something like this"*. Anyone who has been through a crisis and felt God's loving arms wrapped around them knows what I mean. Does this mean that hard times will not ever strike? **No it does not.**

There are teachers who falsely say that all you have to do is to tell God what you want, send in a donation, and all of your health and financial problems will disappear. That is not true. As a matter of fact that is part of what I call ***Fairy Tale Christianity***. There are however, some things that we can be totally assured of. There are some things that God has promised to us. These are the things that we learn from experience that we can depend on. These are the things that I want to discuss in this book.

I know that Christians may sometimes have doubts about their own salvation. It is not unusual for Christians to ask themselves, "Am I really saved?" How can we be certain that we are saved? How can we KNOW that we have done what God requires us to do in order to go to heaven. Let's take a look.

The first question is, how in the world can a person think they are saved when they really are not? How could this be? It gets even scarier when you realize that there are pastors, deacons, and others *getting saved* who have been in church for years. How can this happen? It happens because we live in a world in which Satan is walking around fooling folks. Some people he doesn't have to worry much about. These are the ones he has in the palm of his grubby little hand. The ones who have decided that they want no part of God and that they absolutely will not answer when God calls them. Folks have given up on them, no one is praying for them or witnessing to them. The devil is not worried about that group. I hope you are not in that crowd, and if you are I pray you will get out of it.

There is another group of folks that Satan has to be a little more cautious about. These are the ones who do feel the call of God. These are the ones who are good people, who sit in church year in and year out, and (with Satan's help) believe that they are doing what it takes to satisfy the requirements for Christianity. Yet – these folks are as lost as they can be. In spite of the fact that they are not getting the Gospel of Jesus Christ preached to them, they believe they are on the way to heaven - they have been fooled. How do we know whether or not we are in this category? We do exactly what those folks SHOULD do…we look at the Bible and see what it says about salvation. After we do that, the next step is to see if our profession of faith was genuine and was correct. If it was – we never allow Satan to cause us to question our salvation again. So – let's take a look and decide.

In deciding whether or not you are saved take a look at your motivation for professing Jesus as your Savior. There are reasons that good folks, who have heard the true Gospel preached, might make a "*mistaken*" profession of faith. One reason is because someone is expecting us to do it. If we have family members who have been hounding us to accept the Lord, or a person we are trying to impress it is possible to proclaim Jesus as our Savior even though we don't really even understand what that means. I'd be real surprised if someone in the church I attend found themselves in that particular situation because of the counseling our Pastor conducts before membership. It is possible however, even though there is no intent to deceive.

How do we get saved in the first place?

Let's take a look and see what the Bible says:

<u>#1.</u> We know we must believe[2]. There are folks who are preaching that believing is enough. I'm here to tell you that the Bible says it is not enough.[3] Look what James says about this subject:

James 2:19 *Thou believest that there is one God; thou doest well: the devils also believe, and tremble.*

1. Satan believes in God with a faith that we can not match – but Satan is bound for eternal hellTreat each other with respect

---

2   John 1:12; John 6:29; Acts 16:31; Acts 19:4; 1 John 3:23; 1 John 5: 13
3   Acts 19:15

[4]. He does not claim Jesus as his redeemer[5]. So if believing is not enough, what else is required?

#2. We must recognize that we are sinners[6], and we must repent of our sin[7]. There are lots of scriptures on this subject. There are so many that it is impossible to deny the fact that the Scripture demands our repentance.

#3. When we believe on the Lord Jesus Christ as our Savior, and admit the fact that we are sinners, which requires true repentance – we find that we are forgiven.

> **Note:** There is no way to avoid a little further explanation here, just in case someone is not perfectly clear on how this works. In His wisdom and in His love, God sent His Son Jesus to earth so that Jesus could die on the cross for our sins[8]. Jesus came to earth almost the same way that we all arrived here, He was born. The difference is that Jesus was born of a virgin, Mary[9]. Jesus lived on earth as a man, but he was also God. That is a difficult concept for most of us to understand, and if you need more explanation about any of this, I encourage you to get with someone that you feel comfortable with. At any rate, Jesus died on the cross – and He did it so that we could have eternal salvation. That is the fact that we accept when we accept Jesus as our Lord and Savior. We accept that fact, and we welcome Him into our lives as our Lord.

Is that all there is to it? The answer to that question is YES,

---

4   Revelation 20:10
5   1 Corinthians 12:3
6   Romans 3:23; Romans 5:12;
7   Mark 1:4; Matthew 4:17; Mark 1:4; Mark 1:15; Mark 6:12; Luke 13:3; Luke 15:7; Acts 3:19; Acts 17:30;
8   Of Course – John 3:16
9   Matthew 1:18

that is ALL there is to it. Jesus did the hard part. God made it very easy for us to spend eternity in heaven. Sometimes I think it's too easy. I see un-saved folks in our church sometimes. Some of them are men. When the Pastor gives the invitation, so many times these unsaved men stay right where they are, even though I know that they can feel God calling them for salvation[10]. If the Pastor were to announce that all they had to do to be saved was to climb the highest mountain in North Carolina, they'd do it in a second. The fact that it is so easy – makes it hard for some people. Satan knows that and he uses it to make people ashamed to walk the aisle and accept the free gift of eternal life.

You might say, "I've done all that. Somehow, I still don't feel any different. In fact, some days I don't feel like I'm saved at all". The good news is that feelings have nothing to do with the fact that you are saved. The fact that you just don't feel very Christian-like sometimes is an indicator that you are …………. a human. You are a human who gets discouraged, who hurts, who gets angry and who falls into temptation sometimes. Before you get too excited about that good news, take a look at what else the Bible says:

INDICATORS OF SALVATION

#1. Fruit

Matthew 3:8 *Bring forth therefore fruits meet for repentance:*

Luke 3:8 *Bring forth therefore fruits worthy of repentance, and begin not to say within yourselves, We have Abraham to our father: for I say unto you, That God is able of these stones to raise up children unto Abraham.*

Matthew 7:16 *Ye shall know them by their fruits. Do men gather grapes of thorns, or figs of thistles?*

10   John 6:44

What does that mean? Does that mean that if I do not bring forth good fruit I am not saved? Actually, it is an indicator of your salvation. I think all of us should examine our lives in regards to the above scripture. I'd be amazed if any of us discovered that we were doing such a good job that we had no room for improvement. An honest evaluation might shock us. Do we live Godly lives, spending time with God in prayer and Bible study? Do we put Him first? The question is NOT "are we perfect?" The question is "Are we living a life that would indicate we have truly accepted Jesus as our Master?"

> **NOTE:** Please take a minute and do something you might never have done before. Take a minute to HONESTLY look at yourself and see if you have room for improvement. As a matter of fact – go a little further than that. Make a determination about your own salvation. If you determine you are saved – never – ever let this subject bother you again. If you are unsure, I beg you to speak with someone about it.

#2. Conviction of sin - Christians should <u>not</u> be able to live lives of sin and feel no remorse about it at all. The Holy Spirit lets us know that we are sinning and convicts us that what we are doing is wrong[11].

#3. God gives you His blessed assurance – **Romans 8:16** *The Spirit itself beareth witness with our spirit, that we are the children of God:*

REASONS FOR DOUBT

A person can doubt their salvation because of the fact that they are not living a Christian life. In other words they are backslidden. Don't think for a second that Christians don't

---

11   Romans 8:5; Romans 8:9; Romans 8:13; Romans 8:14;

quench the Holy Spirit and before they know it, find themselves in a backslidden state; and don't make the mistake of thinking it could not possibly happen to you. Once we quit attending church, quit reading our Bible, and quit praying, there is a lot of room for Satan to make himself right at home.

Another reason for doubt is the fact that Satan is on the job – and he is good at what he does. If he can cause us to doubt our salvation he has achieved a great victory. Do not allow him to get away with it. Decide once and for all about your salvation. Make up your mind and never allow the devil to harm you with this subject again. But – keep in mind that there is another reason to feel lost. That reason is that you **are** lost. If that is the case – I urge you to remedy that – right now.

Note: I tried to be extremely careful about how I worded this part of the discussion because I do not want these words to be used by Satan to cause some Christians to doubt their salvation. Rather, I want just the opposite. I want all of us to realize the comfort that comes from the blessed assurance of trusting Jesus Christ as Lord.

Chapter Two

Legalism

When I was a kid I learned Bible stories. Every time I went to Sunday school I learned (or re-learned) about Noah, Moses, Jonah, etc. Sometimes the teacher explained why the story was important and how it pertained to me. Some teachers never did. They simply related the story, made sure we could answer questions and then - we were finished. I grew up knowing the stories pretty well, but I wasn't sure what they had to do with me. That is the wrong answer. Sometimes we read the Bible and just enjoy the story. There is nothing wrong with that. When we study or teach – we should try to relate it to our lives. Why?

2 Timothy 3:16 *All scripture is given by inspiration of God, and is profitable for doctrine, for reproof, for correction, for instruction in righteousness:*

Matthew 7:24 *Therefore whosoever heareth these sayings of mine, and doeth them, I will liken him unto a wise man, which built his house upon a rock:* **25** *And the rain descended, and the floods came, and the winds blew, and beat upon that house; and it fell not: for it was founded upon a rock.* **26** *And every one that heareth these sayings of mine, and doeth them not, shall be likened unto* *a foolish man, which built his house upon the sand:* **27** *And the rain descended, and the floods came, and the winds blew, and beat upon that house; and it fell: and great was the fall of it.*

No matter how rich you are, no matter how good looking you are, and no matter how "lucky" you are…sooner or later you are gong to face a serious crisis in your life. Our Pastor tells us that there are only three types of people in the world. There are those who are going through hard times, those who are coming out of hard times, and those who are about to go through hard times. He is dead on right. In Matthew 7:24-27 Jesus is telling us that we need to be certain that our foundation is solid. We have got to be ready when the bad times hit so that we can stand on our faith. If you are in the middle of a hurricane, it's a bad time to try to build a house. We also know that we wouldn't want to try to weather the storm in a shack that is falling apart. The analogy is that we must have a solid, scriptural, spiritual foundation so that we can cling to the Lord when we need to.

This is an unusual introduction to our topic for this chapter. If you are having a hard time trying to figure out what in the world any of this has to do with legalism, stay with me. Hopefully we'll tie it together. While I don't dwell on it, folks that know me know there was a time that I got away from the Christian walk. Yes – I was a Christian. No – I did not act like one. I'd like to use my situation to explain how legalism can harm. Please do not misunderstand me. I am making no excuses. Anyone who strays from God can blame no one but themselves. I hope my example will be taken in the spirit I'm giving it.

From the time I can remember, I went to church. I went to Sunday school and preaching. I went to the Sunday night version of Sunday school, which we called *Training Union*. Sunday night we went to preaching – again. Tuesday night we had Royal Ambassadors, which is similar to our AWANA program. On Wednesday night we went to the prayer meeting.

When I got older I went to the church youth functions. Every time the door to the church opened, I was there. I was there because I knew that I had to go. It was a rule. (It was the Law.) Don't misunderstand, most of the time I had a good time. I liked most of the things we did, although I didn't get much out of the sermons. My Mom never had to beat me to get me in the car, although I did get in trouble a lot for horsing around in Sunday school and church (Imagine that). I went, I learned the stories and I was a good kid.

The problem was, **I was <u>not</u> going because I loved God and wanted to worship Him.** I was <u>not</u> going so that I could learn Bible principles that would help me with my life's decisions. In fact – no one told me that was the reason I <u>should</u> be there. (When I am in church now, it is to worship God. It is to learn about Him and what He wants of me. It is to hear the words God has given the Preacher. It is to build a foundation so that I'll be ready when (not if) calamity strikes. So that I'll be able to do what God wants me to. And because I enjoy the time spent <u>worshiping God</u> with others.)

When I got old enough to make my own decisions it didn't take me long to realize that no one was going to enforce the rule about going to church. I was away from home, no one would know if I went or not. So gradually, I quit going. And when you quit going to church, no matter what you might argue, it does not take Satan long to get you involved in a lifestyle you should not be involved in.

Here is my point. Anytime we do something <u>just</u> because it is a rule, we are on thin ice. Imagine praying – <u>just</u> because you know the Bible says you should. Imagine reading the Bible – <u>just</u> because you were told it was expected. Certainly there are times we pray or read the Bible when we are not really in the mood. I know there are times when I leave the house to come to church when I don't have an attitude of worship. But (you get the point) – our <u>motivation</u> should <u>not</u> be the rules (Law).

Am I saying that we no longer have to obey the Laws of the Old Testament? **I am not.** I am saying that even if we had never heard of the Ten Commandments we should live a life in which we did not violate them – because of our love of the Lord and our desire to please Him. Let's look at some scripture.

Luke 11:46 *And he said, Woe unto you also, ye lawyers! for ye lade men with burdens grievous to be borne, and ye yourselves touch not the burdens with one of your fingers.*

Luke 11:52 *Woe unto you, lawyers! for ye have taken away the key of knowledge: ye entered not in yourselves, and them that were entering in ye hindered.*

As much as I would love it if this were a universal condemnation of all lawyers, it is not. Jesus is telling the Pharisees that they have gotten stupid with their legalistic ways. He is telling them two things. One, it has gotten to the point that there are so many rules that it is not only grievous, but it is impossible to keep them. The second point Jesus is making is that the keeping of the law has become the goal. The Pharisees are not interested in worship. They want to be seen by men as something special. In other words their motive is the attention of man, not the worship of God.

> **NOTE**: I think a good way to explain this is to look at **Eddy Haskell**, from the old *Leave it to Beaver* television show. Whenever Eddy was around adults he was a model kid. He would ask them how they were doing, and would always compliment Mrs. Cleaver on her dress or her hair. He acted exactly the way we'd love for any of our kids to act. The problem was, everyone saw right through Eddy. They knew his motivation. He was telling them what he thought they wanted to hear, so he would look good. Now – was what Eddy said wrong? Of course it wasn't. Should he have acted that way? Yes, it was

> perfectly appropriate. What made it inappropriate then? The fact that Eddy was saying those things not to "honor" the adult he was speaking with, but to "honor" himself. That is also what the Pharisees were doing. They were fooling themselves, other people, and attempting to fool God. God did not buy it[12].

Luke 16:15 *And he said unto them, Ye are they which justify yourselves before men; but God knoweth your hearts: for that which is highly esteemed among men is abomination in the sight of God.* **16** *The law and the prophets were until John: since that time the kingdom of God is preached, and every man presseth into it.* **17** *And it is easier for heaven and earth to pass, than one tittle of the law to fail[13].*

God's standards do not change – ever. The Law still holds. However, God knows that there is no way we could keep the Law, and thankfully He gave us another way. He sent His Son Jesus to die on the cross for us. All we have to do is to accept that free gift in order to be saved. But – He still expects us to keep the rules. The question here is, what is your motivation for keeping them?

Liberalism   Scripture and the Love of God   Legalism

Look at the little drawing. All the way to the left we have liberalism. At the far left there are teachings that totally contradict the Word of God. Ideas like "You don't really need to accept Jesus, as long as you are a good person". As we creep closer along the line, towards the circle the ideas get a little less

---

12   Luke 11: 41-44
13   Also see Matthew 5:18

radical, but they are still not scriptural. We get ideas like, "You don't really need to go to church to worship God".

Once we enter the circle we get into the scriptures and doing what God wants us to, because we love Him and want to do what is right. We still obey the Laws He has given us, but the obedience of the Law is a product of our love for Him, not a goal unto it's self. There are still disagreements inside the circle. Most of these disagreements have to do with the type of music that is played, or something along those lines. Even inside the circle we have our opinions as to what is too liberal and what is too legalistic. But we are <u>always</u> in accordance with the Word of God.

As we continue to the right we start getting outside the circle. This is when we get in trouble again. When we first leave the circle we get into rules that seem harmless but that are simply not scriptural. This is where we get ideas like "Women can't wear pants, make-up, or jewelry". (It seems like these rules are always about women.) On the very far right we get into ideas like, "If you are in the will of God you should be able to drink poison and handle rattle snakes without being harmed"[14]. As long as we are in the circle we are OK. Once we stray either way, we have a problem.

BOTTOM LINE

We do not want to be anything like the Pharisees. We want our motivations to be correct. If I had been going to church for the right reason, I would never have quit going. Every time we teach a child a Bible story we should tell them how it relates to them. Otherwise it is just another story, just another *fairy tale*. Every class we have, every sermon we hear, we should try to see how it could relate to our lives. Our goal should be to learn so that we're ready to do what God wants us to do, and so that we are prepared for trying times. Our goal should be to <u>get our children</u> to go to church because they love God. That

14   They get this from verses like Mark 16:18.

is scriptural. As adults we have a certain obligation to make things interesting for a child, so that they will enjoy it as well. As Christian adults we also have an obligation make them go to church on days they don't want to. The lesson here, and the challenge, is to find the right combination. Just remember this – anytime we start making "written in stone" decisions about the way we should act, we should always be sure we are acting in accordance with the Bible. We should also look at our motivation. And somewhere in there – there's room for a little sprinkling of the common sense that God has given us.

Chapter Three

Should you quit your church?

Let me start this chapter off by asking you, "Have you ever considered quitting the church you are a member of? If not – I'd like to encourage you to please take a moment and consider it. (We'll come back to this question at the end of the chapter.) When you decide that you need to find a church to join there are certain steps we to take. Let's look at them:

Step 1 - <u>Make certain you have educated yourself as completely as possible about the church</u>. The analogy of a marriage partnership fits very well here. When you first start to date someone (assuming that you like them), everything is wonderful. Guys think to themselves, "This is great. I have finally met someone who does not have **any** flaws at all. She does not even mind when I get lost, and never bugs me to stop and ask directions". The female thinks to herself, "What a wonderful fellow. He never says a word when I am late. He appears to be perfect". All of us know that this is the fairy tale part of the new romance. We know that it takes time for a couple to really get to know one another. We know that if they rush into a life long relationship without taking time to learn as much as possible about each other, there is a good chance the relationship will fail.

When looking for a local church, we should take care to be certain that we do not make that same kind of mistake. Most churches require potential members to go through an interview process. This is a good time to ask questions about the church. You should ask for a copy of their constitution, by laws and any other documents that you feel would help you in making your decision. It goes without saying that the very first thing that you should ascertain is whether or not the church is a Bible believing, Bible preaching church. How do we do this? We do this by knowing the Word of God and being prepared to test everything we hear against scripture. Also – ask them! After you've asked your questions, stick around and get to know them a little better, just like you would a potential spouse.

Step 2 – <u>Make certain that when you join a church, you are doing what God wants you to do</u>.   We'll continue the analogy of a marriage partnership. It goes without saying that a Christian should spend a lot of time in prayer about who they should marry. It's hard to believe that anyone would purposely wed anyone if they thought it was the opposite of what God wanted them to do. After praying and making sure that the person we are going to marry is the person God wants us to marry, it's time to take a walk down the aisle. Here's the point – we make sure we know what we are getting into and that it is God's will…then we make the commitment.

Step 2.5 – <u>If at anytime you are dating (or looking for a church), and you feel you've made a mistake – bail out</u>. Imagine you've been dating this person for about six months. You are starting to feel pretty comfortable with each other. In other words you are starting to see the real person. You start to see some things that you didn't see before, mainly because the other person kept them hidden from you. You go out to a nice (or even a crummy) restaurant and the person you are with belches really loud – and then laughs even louder. You think to yourself, "there is no way in the world I can marry a girl who is this crude." (No offense Becky) You decide to tell the person that they need to find someone else, that you are not interested. Do you know what you have done wrong? You have done NOTHING wrong. That is what the dating part is for, so that you can get to know someone.

When we are looking for a church to commit to we should take the same precautions. The church lady who was so sweet to you might turn out to be someone you just can not deal with. You might realize that there is something else about the church that you just are not comfortable with. At that point it makes sense for you to keep looking.

> **NOTE:** When we are dating, for the purpose of meeting someone to spend our lives with – what do we do? When you reach a point where you are ready to settle down, and you meet someone who you think might be right, you don't keep shopping. You stay with that person and make sure. I'm not sure why we can't do the same thing when we are looking for a Church to join. If the first one we visit is the one we fall in love with, what is the point in looking elsewhere?

Step 3 – <u>Make the commitment</u>. Once you are sure you are in God's will and that you have found a church where you can serve as well as be ministered to, make the commitment. But remember – it is a commitment. Now when your husband belches in public you can't just tell him to hit the road. When you wake up and you are upset with your wife because she couldn't care less that the light she just turned on woke you up, that is not a reason to split. As a matter of fact, in a scriptural marriage the thought of divorce should not even enter our head.

Likewise, when we are in a church that God has led us to, we should not even think of leaving when we get upset. I did say "when" and not "if", because we are going to get upset sometime – I guarantee you. Someone is going to make you mad. Realize now that no one is married for long without getting extremely angry with their husband or wife. As a matter of fact they can make you angrier than just about anyone else can. We are going to get our feelings hurt in church sometime. Quitting is the wrong answer.

NOTE: Does that mean that you should **never** quit a church that you are a member of? No it does not. There are certain times (just as in marriage), that you should consider leaving. <u>Examples</u>: The church gets away from scripture – or – you <u>truly</u> feel that you have made a mistake and this is not where God wants you – or –after a time in the church you feel God is calling you to serve elsewhere. These are only a few examples.

Chapter Four

Death (& Life)

1Corinthians 15:55 *O <u>death, where</u> is <u>thy</u> <u>sting?</u> O <u>grave,</u> <u>where</u> is <u>thy</u> <u>victory?</u>*

Ken Hankins used to say, "Every one of us, if we live long enough, is gonna die". The statistics are that one out of every one person dies. If you look at the figures on death over a seventy year period you find that they are not affected at all by major wars or natural disasters. The amount of people who died over that period does not change. This is true even when whole villages or cities are wiped out.

Every person I know has been saddened by the death of someone. We know from our personal experiences that death strikes every age, from infants to the very elderly. Life is a precious possession that we all hang on to, but the fact is, we all know that we are eventually going to die[15]. Our eventual death is a fact we have to live with. This chapter is really about death from two different perspectives. The loss of those we love, and our own eventual demise.

Before I met my wife Mindi, I was dating a girl I thought that I would end up spending my life with. We had gone together for a little over three years when (and I know you're <u>gonna find this </u>hard to believe), she decided she'd be happier

15   Hebrews 9:27

if I was not around. That's just about the way she worded it too. After she got rid of me she started seeing other guys. I ran into her at a party and she had her new boyfriend with her. As she stood there oozing joy, she notified me that she had never been happier in her life. Hearing that just about killed me. I was thinking, "I'm so glad I was able to brighten up your life a little – by getting out of it. I hope this guy turns out to be a wife beater".

Now from a logical point of view I should have thought, "I love you and as long as you are happy, that is all that matters to me". That is not the way it works. And that is not the way it works when a Christian loved one dies. Even though we know that they are so much better off, and logically we should be bubbling over with happiness, we still feel that dreadful loss. We are still overcome with grief. Why do we feel that way if our loved one is so much better off in heaven? …<u>Because we are human beings with human feelings.</u> And we miss them. We are not sorry for them, we are sorry for us. And that is perfectly natural.

The good news is that the Holy Spirit is there to comfort us[16]. This is a gift that is unique to Christians[17].   There are many stories in my church of folks who have experienced the tragic loss of loved ones - being comforted by the presence of the Holy Spirit. Does that mean there are no tears or that the grief disappears? **OF COURSE NOT**. It means that we will not face it alone. I often repeat that we need to pray and prepare <u>now</u> so that we'll be ready to face the tragedies that we <u>will</u> face during our lifetime. We should prepare ourselves during the good times for the difficult times that every single one of us <u>is</u> going to experience. Christ is the joy of our lives. He is also our comfort during heartbreak.

What about our own death? How do we face that? We had a great example in our Sunday school class. One of our <u>faithful members</u>, Gordon Williams was dieing of cancer. He

16   John 16:7; John 14:16
17   Ecclesiastics 4:1

and his wife Bonnie had accepted that fact. Gordon's time was limited. They openly discussed it and, although it was something they dreaded, they had the peace and the joy of knowing that Gordon would be in heaven the split second he left us.

Quick Story

Bonnie told me this story shortly before Gordon died. She was talking to Gordon and he said, "I wish you could go with me". Bonnie replied, "Well, if it's the Lord's will I might". Gordon said, "If I go first I'll wait for you". Then he added, "I can't wait to see all my friends and be able to run around with them up there." Bonnie looked at me and laughed and said, "I knew he wouldn't be up there just waiting".

Bonnie and Gordon talked about this event openly. They knew that although this is an incredibly sad chapter in the book that is the love story of Bonnie and Gordon, it is not the last chapter. (In the last chapter they get to see each other again.)

That is the amazing promise that Easter reminds us of. Jesus did face death on the cross for our sins. But he arose after three days and is in heaven right now. Some day, <u>if</u> we accept the sacrifice he made for us, we will join him. <u>With that in mind we have two very obvious responsibilities. The first one is to put our faith and trust in Jesus Christ as our Savior.</u> If you haven't done that – do it now. If you're not sure how to do it, ask. The sad reality is that we take more time trying to figure out what to wear to church than we do worrying about how we'll spend eternity.

Some Christians teach that, because we are Christians, and the person who died was a Christian, we should somehow be happy they're dead - happy they're in heaven - happy they're with the Lord and therefore sorrow is prohibited. You will not find that in the Bible.

The Bible clearly defines great men of God, men full of faith mourning the loss of their loved ones. **Genesis 23:2** *And Sarah died in Kirjatharba; the same is Hebron in the land of Canaan: and Abraham came to mourn for Sarah, and to weep for her.* Abraham was close to the Lord; still the death of his wife hurt him greatly. **Genesis 24:67** says *And Isaac brought her into his mother Sarah's tent, and took Rebekah, and she became his wife; and he loved her: and Isaac was comforted after his mother's death.* This was three years after his mother's death. There is no suggestion that Isaac should have "gotten over it" immediately after the funeral.

Some folks might ask, doesn't the Bible teach that the Christian is not to grieve over death? **1 Thessalonians 4:13** *But I would not have you to be ignorant, brethren, concerning them which are asleep, that ye sorrow not, even as others which have no hope.* The verse does not say we are not to sorrow, but that we are not to sorrow as though there is no hope. Of course we should to be glad our loved ones are saved. Of course we are comforted by their presence with the Lord. But for crying out loud – we still miss them. If you are asking, "Where was God the day my loved one died?" The answer is that He was, and is in, exactly the same place He was the day <u>His</u> beloved Son died. God cares about our grief[18].

The second obligation we have is to witness to others, including our loved ones. How do we do that? We pray for them, asking the Holy Spirit to begin ministering in their lives. We ask others to help us. We live a life that will be a Christian example. Although we don't badger them, we do have to realize that we might very well have to face the fact that they (and we) might have to experience a little discomfort in order to witness to them.

If we saw someone trapped in a car that was about to catch fire we'd do whatever it took to get them out. We'd break windows, cut seat belts, yell for help, scream for someone to

---

18   Isaiah 53:4

call 911, etc. We'd put our own lives at risk, for a complete stranger. Why are we so afraid to merely talk to someone we love about something that is so much more hazardous than a car fire?

Easter is the perfect opportunity to witness. Just about everyone celebrates Easter in some manner or other, even if it is just with a day off. It opens the door for us to talk about the resurrection with them. None of us will be here in 60 or 70 years – but – <u>we will be somewhere</u>. We should all make a pledge. We should decide that we are not going to lose another friend without being able to say, "That is someone I witnessed to". (We should do this even if all we are able to do is just invite them to church.) Hopefully we'll be able to add, "I led them to the Lord".

Chapter Five

Hypocrites

As part of my checkered past I was a firefighter working on the ambulance. One good thing about driving an ambulance is that you get a lot of stories. My Sunday school class wonders why - if I have so many stories - they have to hear the same ones over and over. Here's one of them:

There was a house that I used to drive by a lot. It was a brick house with an exceptionally well groomed yard. The house always looked great and there was no reason to believe that it was anything other than perfectly normal on the inside. We got an ambulance call to that house one day and found out that things were far from average on the inside. An elderly lady lived in the house with her son. The son was about forty years old and he was mentally retarded. I used to see him around town a lot cutting grass and doing yard work for people. He was a big guy and looked kind of like a pitiful Hoss Cartwright. If you are too young to know who Hoss is – keep it to yourself please.

Anyway, one day my partner and I got an ambulance call to the house. The dispatcher was not sure what the problem was. When we arrived and knocked on the door the retarded man, I believe his name was Tommy, answered. He was crying and having a difficult time talking to us. He kept telling us that there was something wrong with his mother. If that were all there was to it this wouldn't be much of a story. There are a couple of more facts that I need to make you aware of. When he opened that front door, I almost passed out from the smell. I could be wrong but I don't believe I have ever smelled anything so gross in my life. Folks that know me know that I have a pretty weak stomach. I was standing at the front door gagging so hard that I didn't know what I was gonna do.

There was one more minor problem. The house was full of dogs. There were probably 25-30 dogs in the house and every one of them was trying to get out to bite me. I had a partner, but I'm sure the dogs were trying to bite **me**. Anyway, poor old Tommy was finally able to herd all of the dogs into the back yard and my partner and I entered the house. When we got inside we saw where the stench was coming from. The entire floor was covered with newspaper. When I say the entire floor, I mean the **ENTIRE FLOOR**. The newspaper was covered with every body function that a dog is capable of performing. We were slipping, trying not to fall down while we made our way into the mother's bedroom. She was still alive, but had had a stroke. We took her to the hospital, she lived, and we reported the living conditions we had found to the health department.

If I hadn't been to that house that night I would have continued to think that it was a normal dwelling and was clean inside. I would have believed this even though I drove by that house several times a week. There was no way for me to tell by looking at the outside. I had to get inside that house to know. People are the same way. We can see them at church, acting pious and not have any idea who the real person is. The only way to know is to get inside that person – and <u>only God can do that</u>. So the point here is that while we will be able to define what a hypocrite is, the truth of the matter is that God is the only one who is going to know for sure. As a matter of fact our obligation in this matter is to make sure that **we** are not the hypocrites!

We often talk about the fact that a lot of folks use, "there are too many hypocrites there," as an excuse not to go to church. I've been thinking about that quite a bit. Besides the obvious weakness of that particular excuse – what exactly is a hypocrite? (Is it any sinner ………………... other than us?) Can two people live parallel lives of sin all week and then come to church, and one is a hypocrite while the other is just a sinner? If so, then what is the difference?

Well, you probably guessed this by now – we're going to check with the Bible and see what God's Word says on this subject. (Imagine that)

The Greek word for hypocrite is pronounced **_hoo-ok-ree-tace'_**. It means**: an actor** under an assumed character (stage player), i.e. (figuratively) a dissembler. Since a person who is playing an assumed character **knows** he is playing an assumed character, we can surmise that a hypocrite **knows** he is acting a role. There is of course, no way that we can really know what a person is truly like – most of the time…and therein lies our problem. OK, it has been several paragraphs and it's about time to introduce some scripture. Not only does the Bible address the issue of hypocrisy, but as a matter of fact Jesus thought it was important enough to address it at length.

Matthew 15: **8.** *This people draweth nigh unto me with their mouth, and honoureth me with their lips; but their heart is far from me.* **9** *But in vain they do worship me, teaching for doctrines the commandments of men.*

I believe this verse contains the key to the whole thing. Jesus is talking about the scribes and Pharisees, but he is also talking about us. In **_verse 8_** He tells us that these guys talk big, but they do not have the desire to worship God in their hearts. These are the folks who come to church and are saying, "Look at me, look how good I am. Look at me, I teach a Sunday school class. Look at me…." These folks talk the talk, but they are not present in church to truly worship and to honor God. Now I don't know about you, but there are many times when I feel like a hypocrite. There are lots of times when I think to myself, "How am I worthy to stand in front of a group of good people and attempt to lead them in a class?" What makes me any different than the Pharisees?

Here is the difference. Jesus is not saying that He is upset with these guys because they are **sinners**. He is saying it is what is in your heart that makes the difference. If we come to church for our own purposes, so that we can feel good about ourselves and let others look at us, we are displaying symptoms of hypocrisy. If we come to church with the attitude that we deserve to be here because we are so good, and that it kind of hacks us a little that somehow or another a couple of sinners got in, we're wrong. The danger here is that all of us sin and as a result – sometimes we feel like a hypocrite just having the nerve to show up at church. We might feel that way because we didn't act like a Christian all week, and then have the nerve to show up at church. It's my belief that feeling that way is one of the indications that a person is not a hypocrite.

I just said that Jesus was not upset with these guys for sinning. Let's take a look at how Jesus handled one sinner before we continue on with His encounters with frauds. This is a well known passage:

John 8: 1. *Jesus went unto the mount of Olives.* 2. *And early in the morning he came again into the temple, and all the people came unto him; and he sat down, and taught them.* 3. *And the scribes and Pharisees brought unto him a woman taken in adultery; and when they had set her in the midst,* 4. *They say unto him, Master, this woman was taken in adultery, in the very act.* 5. *Now Moses in the law commanded us, that such should be stoned: but what sayest thou?* 6. *This they said, tempting him, that they might have to accuse him. But Jesus stooped down, and with his finger wrote on the ground, as though he heard them not.*

7. So when they continued asking him, he lifted up himself, and said unto them, He that is without sin among you, let him first cast a stone at her. **8.** *And again he stooped down, and wrote on the ground.* **9.** *And they which heard it, being convicted by their own conscience, went out one by one, beginning at the eldest, even unto the last: and Jesus was left alone, and the woman standing in the midst.* **10.** *When Jesus had lifted up himself, and saw none but the woman, he said unto her, Woman, where are those thine accusers? hath no man condemned thee?* **11.** *She said, No man, Lord. And Jesus said unto her, Neither do I condemn thee: go, and sin no more.*

The Pharisees bought that woman to Jesus for two reasons. The first reason was that they had caught her in the act of adultery. That was a pretty serious offense in those days. It was serious enough that if you were caught you were put to death. As a matter of fact they still do that in several Middle Eastern countries. The second reason they bought the woman to Jesus was to test (or tempt) Him. They wanted to see how He would handle this very difficult situation.

Here are the facts. This lady was a sinner. Not only was she a sinner, but she was a pretty bad sinner. She had committed an act that was considered appalling. And here she was in front of Jesus. Surely He would condemn her. Much to their surprise and I'm sure, their embarrassment, Jesus did not condemn this woman. Instead Jesus pointed out the sin in the lives of these "righteous" men. I could be wrong, but I've always felt that some of the men who were present that day had participated in the act of adultery with this very woman. (That's not scriptural – it's just the way I feel.) Jesus shamed them because they were absolute hypocrites. And then he forgave that woman. I believe that if Jesus had found this same woman in church, acting pious and condemning others, He would have set her straight. Why? Because she would have been living an un-repentant lie.

This brings us to an interesting point. Can two men live

parallel lives of sin, and be judged differently? What if two guys, we'll call them Larry and Moe spent their Saturday night drinking in two different bars, in two different towns. Both of them got equally drunk, and both of them went home with a woman who was not their wife. The next day both of them went to church and sat in Sunday school and Church. Both of them sang the same songs, both of them prayed out loud, both of them went to the altar and knelt down during the invitation. Is it possible that God is looking at them differently? The answer is that it is absolutely possible that God would look at them differently. One of them could be there with a broken heart, begging the Lord for forgiveness and grieving about what he had done. The other might be there saying to himself, "I hope everyone can see me OK. I really need to keep up appearances." Remember when Jesus said "*but their heart is far from me*"? That's the difference in these two guys.

LET'S TAKE ANOTHER LOOK AT JESUS AND THE HYPOCRITES.

Matthew 23. 1. *Then spake Jesus to the multitude, and to his disciples,* **2.** *Saying, The scribes and the Pharisees sit in Moses' seat:* **3.** *All therefore whatsoever they bid you observe, that observe and do; but do not ye after their works: for they say, and do not.* **4.** *For they bind heavy burdens and grievous to be borne, and lay them on men's shoulders; but they themselves will not move them with one of their fingers.* **5.** *But all their works they do for to be seen of men: they make broad their phylacteries, and enlarge the borders of their garments,* **6.** *And love the uppermost rooms at feasts, and the chief seats in the synagogues,* **7.** *And greetings in the markets, and to be called of men, Rabbi, Rabbi.*

The thread runs true in this passage in which Jesus speaks about the scribes and the Pharisees. He is simply saying that they say one thing and do another. Everything they do is so that men will see it and praise <u>them</u>. Their motivation and their heart is what makes them hypocrites. As you read the Bible you can read over and over again of the compassion that Jesus shows for sinners. Even on the cross He prayed "*forgive them; for they know not what they do.*" Think of that. The quivering mass that was the human body of Jesus was on the cross, suffering like few have ever suffered. His words to His Father were a plea for forgiveness for the very men who had done this to Him. There is no anger – only compassion. None of this compassion is present when it comes to the hypocritical Pharisees. Why? The answer I believe is because they knew what was right, pretended to do it, and attempted to fool people. Look at the following passage:

Matthew 23: 13 *But woe unto you, scribes and Pharisees, hypocrites! for ye shut up the kingdom of heaven against men: for ye neither go in yourselves, neither suffer ye them that are entering to go in.* **14.** *Woe unto you, scribes and Pharisees, hypocrites! for ye devour widows' houses, and for a pretence make long prayer: therefore ye shall receive the greater damnation.* **15.** *Woe unto you, scribes and Pharisees, hypocrites! for ye compass sea and land to make one proselyte, and when he is made, ye make him twofold more the child of hell than yourselves.*

23. *Woe unto you, scribes and Pharisees, hypocrites! for ye pay tithe of mint and anise and cummin, and have omitted the weightier matters of the law, judgment, mercy, and faith: these ought ye to have done, and not to leave the other undone.*

24. *Ye blind guides, which strain at a gnat, and swallow a camel.* **25.** *Woe unto you, scribes and Pharisees, hypocrites! for ye make clean the outside of the cup and of the platter, but within they are full of extortion and excess.* **26.** *Thou blind Pharisee, cleanse first that which is within the cup and platter, that the outside of them may be clean also.*

27. *Woe unto you, scribes and Pharisees, hypocrites! for ye are like unto whited sepulchres, which indeed appear beautiful outward, but are within full of dead men's bones, and of all uncleanness.* **28.** *Even so ye also outwardly appear righteous unto men, but within ye are full of hypocrisy and iniquity.* **29.** *Woe unto you, scribes and Pharisees, hypocrites! because ye build the tombs of the prophets, and garnish the sepulchres of the righteous,* **30.** *And say, If we had been in the days of our fathers, we would not have been partakers with them in the blood of the prophets.* **31.** *Wherefore ye be witnesses unto yourselves, that ye are the children of them which killed the prophets.* **32.** *Fill ye up then the measure of your fathers.* **33.** *Ye serpents, ye generation of vipers, how can ye escape the damnation of hell?* **34.** *Wherefore, behold, I send unto you prophets, and wise men, and scribes: and some of them ye shall kill and crucify; and some of them shall ye scourge in your synagogues, and persecute them from city to city:*

Listen to the difference in the way that Jesus addresses these guys and the way he speaks about "ordinary" sinners.

Matthew 9: 10. *And it came to pass, as Jesus sat at meat in the house, behold, many publicans and sinners came and sat down with him and his disciples.* **11.** *And when the Pharisees saw it, they said unto his disciples, Why eateth your Master with publicans and sinners?* **12.** *But when Jesus heard that, he said unto them, They that be whole need not a physician, but they that are sick.* **13.** *But go ye and learn what that meaneth, I will have mercy, and not sacrifice: for I am not come to call the righteous, but sinners to repentance.*

Bottom Line

There is story after story in the Bible about the love and the compassion that Jesus has for sinners. In fact, the whole reason for His coming to earth was so that we could be forgiven.

There is not one place in the Bible where Jesus shows anything but the utmost contempt for hypocrites. What is the lesson here? Actually there are several. One is that we had better be sure that when we worship God – we are sincere. When I read the Bible it is very clear to me that God does not like false motivation AT ALL. The second lesson here is that all of us are going to sin. <u>All of us are going to sin.</u> When you approach God with true repentance, asking for forgiveness, that is NOT hypocrisy. The third lesson here is that under normal circumstances we can't guess another person's motives. It is not our place to judge them. I don't know about you, but it takes everything I have to keep myself straight. I do not have time to set in church and try to make a list of who is and who is not sincere in their worship. I'll tell you this though – I will do everything in my power to try to keep myself out of the "hypocrite mode". I can not imagine hearing the words that the Pharisees heard – from Jesus.

Chapter Six

The Impossible to Tame Tongue

Kids can bring an unbelievable amount of joy into our lives. Every age my kids have ever been – has been my favorite. I know I need to be very careful about trying to second guess God, but I do think I have an idea that would have made life a lot easier for all of us. I wish the Lord had fixed it so that kids did not grow a tongue until they were twenty one years old. Not only would my life be a lot easier, but my kids would have a better chance of **making** it to twenty one. This chapter is about our life long struggle with that little bitty part of our body that is so difficult to control.

James 3: 1. *My brethren, be not many masters, knowing that we shall receive the greater condemnation.* **2.** *For in many things we offend all. If any man offend not in word, the same is a perfect man, and able also to bridle the whole body.* **3.** *Behold, we put bits in the horses' mouths, that they may obey us; and we turn about their whole body.* **4.** *Behold also the ships, which though they be so great, and are driven of fierce winds, yet are they turned about with a very small helm, whithersoever the governor listeth.* **5.** *Even so the tongue is a little member, and boasteth great things. Behold, how great a matter a little fire kindleth!* **6.** *And the tongue is a fire, a world of iniquity:*

so is the tongue among our members, that it defileth the whole body, and setteth on fire the course of nature; and it is set on fire of hell. **7.** *For every kind of beasts, and of birds, and of serpents, and of things in the sea, is tamed, and hath been tamed of mankind:* **8.** *But the tongue can no man tame; it is an unruly evil, full of deadly poison.* **9.** *Therewith bless we God, even the Father; and therewith curse we men, which are made after the similitude of God.* **10.** *Out of the same mouth proceedeth blessing and cursing. My brethren, these things ought not so to be.* **11.** *Doth a fountain send forth at the same place sweet water and bitter?* **12.** *Can the fig tree, my brethren, bear olive berries? either a vine, figs? so can no fountain both yield salt water and fresh.*

As we've discussed many times, Satan is an expert at fooling us[19]. He has a lot of tools in his chest, and a whole bunch of them involve speaking. Let's take a look at some of them.

CURSING

I have known (and still do know) a number of Christians who make no effort at all to <u>not</u> curse. For some reason, they don't think they need to worry about it. I'm not speaking about someone hitting their thumb and yelling something out (although all of us know we shouldn't do that either) – I'm talking about folks who regularly sprinkle profanity into their routine conversations. This is a sin[20]. Cussing is, in and of it's self – a sin; however it goes further than that. Like so many of the other actions we look at in this book, cursing can destroy our witness. That is also a sin[21].

---

19   Revelation 12:9

20   Romans 3:14; Matthew 15:11; Matthew 15:18; Luke 6:45; Ephesians 4:29; Colossians 3:8;

21   Romans 14:21; 1 Corinthians 8:12

NOTE: There are some habits that folks suffer with all of their lives. When a person becomes a Christian all of their problems and all of their addictions do not just disappear as if by magic. We know that the Lord can and will give us help to defeat <u>any</u> sin that might haunt us. The fact of the matter is that having a habitual foul mouth is not that difficult a habit to stop. Some folks will suffer and will continue to suffer all of their lives with certain types of addictions. I do not see how anyone can argue that they have an addiction to profanity and that they can not stop[22]! That is weak, and anyone who habitually uses foul language and has no qualms whatsoever about it needs to spend some time thinking and praying about it[23].

GOSSIP

There is an old joke about a lady who was coming out of church. She asked her husband, "Do you think that Jones lady is tinting her hair?" "I didn't even see her," admitted Mr. Smith. "And that dress Mrs. Henderson was wearing," continued his wife, "Really, don't tell me you think that's the proper costume for a mother of three." "I'm afraid I didn't notice that either," said the husband. "Oh, for heaven's sake," snapped his wife. "A lot of good it does **you** to go to church."

Man, sometimes I wish gossip was not against the rules – but it is. It is so easy to get caught up in the trap of talking bad about someone. Since I know this is wrong, I usually try to start off by saying something like "I know I probably should not tell you this but…" (Like that makes it OK.) Telling harmful tales about someone is not scriptural[24]. **Ephesians**

---

22   James 1:26
23   Philippians 4:13
24   Ephesians 4:31

4:31 *Let all bitterness, and wrath, and anger, and clamour, and evil speaking, be put away from you, with all malice:*

Is there ever a time when it is OK to tell something bad about someone? There are times when the circumstances might dictate that we relate a bad story about another person. For example, what if you knew that someone was about to lend me their golf clubs and you knew it would be a mistake? Let's pretend that you had loaned me something a few months earlier and I had never returned it. Not only that, but you found out that I had sold it and kept the money. Don't you think you would have an obligation to tell the potential lender so that they would not get burned?

That can lead to another problem; **sometimes we rationalize** that we have a good reason to tell tales. We can pretend to ourselves that our motive is pure and that we have someone else's interest at heart. As Ken Hankins has said so many times, it is all about motive. Someone in our Sunday school class mentioned the fact that we even use prayer as an excuse to gossip. When we say "Pray for so and so, she has a real drinking problem," what we really mean is "Can you believe little Miss Goody Two Shoes? She drinks like a fish."

Sometimes the temptation to talk about someone is powerful. It is very difficult to control at times, especially if the gossip is 100% truth. When we have interesting tidbits about someone in our church who is in a position of authority the temptation is even greater. Christians should be held accountable, but there are scriptural means in place to take care of these occasions. Here is the bottom line on gossip – we should not do it. How do we know when we can/ should tell on someone? Truthfully and honestly consider the motive, keeping in mind that we can fool ourselves, but we can't fool the Lord. Take a look at the scriptures on this subject and then consider the good or bad that can come from it. It's usually not difficult to decide whether or not it is right.

FAILURE TO SPEAK[25]

James 4:17 *Therefore to him that knoweth to do good, and doeth it not, to him it is sin.*

This is just the opposite of what we just discussed; sometimes not having control of our tongue means that we do <u>not</u> speak when we <u>should</u>. Try as we might we cannot make ourselves speak up. If we are in a group of people and they are making fun of someone who they know is a Christian – <u>because</u> that person is a Christian – do we speak up and say "Listen, whatever you think about them, think about me too. I love Jesus and I go to church and I pray and I am not at all ashamed[26]?" There might be other times that we don't say anything, not because we are ashamed of Jesus, but because we are ashamed of the way we live our lives. We realize that if we speak up and announce that we are a Christian we would look pretty silly. The answer for that problem is so obvious it needs no comment[27].

CHURCH DISSENTION

I've done a lot of reading on the subject of what causes churches to split. It really is an amazing subject. If I had to pick one word that summed it up I'd pick "pride". Most of the things that true Christians disagree on are just plain stupid. Ideally we would all agree on everything[28]. There are really two types of disagreements that we get into. One involves matters of business. Should we buy a bus, build a gym, or hire a grounds keeper? The second area of disagreement is in the area <u>of doctrine. I've</u> found that in both cases the disagreements

25   James 4:17
26   Mark 8:38; Luke 9:26; Romans 1:16; Romans 9:33; Romans 10:11; 2 Timothy 1:8;
27   2 Timothy 2:15
28   1 Corinthians 1:10

are normally very juvenile. Someone will read this and say, "How can you say that disagreements over doctrine are not important[29]? We should agree on everything that the Bible says!" Listen; there are obvious matters that we <u>can not</u> disagree on. At this stage of the game all of us should know what those are: virgin birth of Christ, His resurrection after three days, manner of salvation, etc. There are other topics that, while they matter – should <u>not</u> be church splitters. There are a lot of points in the Bible that call for opinion. What are some areas we can disagree on? What color was a certain person, what did someone do for a living, even who wrote a certain book. I believe that the sin comes in when we elevate these arguments to a point that they <u>do</u> start to matter and they start to hurt. They start to hurt us, our church and our walk with the Lord. I like to argue my point as much (probably more) than anyone (except David Rose). The problem comes when we can't let it go and when we start to get angry over the subject[30].

BOTTOM LINE

Pastor Ken had a saying that I like a lot. He used to say that you can tell what is in a vessel by what spills out when you upset it. You can also tell what is in a person by what spills out when you upset them. Profanity is a habit – one that no Christian should tolerate in themselves. Gossip, and church dissention are also behaviors that are not scriptural – no matter how tempting (or how much fun) they may be. Even harder sometimes is getting that tongue to speak up when it should. The thing just does not want to cooperate – ever.

The good news is that God knew this and that is why it is discussed in scripture so much. Let's face it – of all of the addictions that we can be cursed with – there really is no excuse (most of the time) for failure to control our speech. As in all things, prayer is the key to whipping this particular

29   Titus 3:9; 2 Timothy 2:23
30   1 Corinthians 11:16; Philippians 2:3

problem. When all is said and done the responsibility still lies square on our shoulders.

James 1:19 *Wherefore, my beloved brethren, let every man be swift to hear, slow to speak, slow to wrath:*

Chapter Seven

Anger
(That makes me mad)

Anger is a funny (not really) thing. Everyone gets angry. Very few people live lives that are not influenced <u>at all</u> by it. For many people it is a burden that threatens their personal relationships. Anger causes so much harm and so much damage, and yet all of us get angry. Even God gets angry.

Joshua 7:1 *But the children of Israel committed a trespass in the accursed thing: for Achan, the son of Carmi, the son of Zabdi, the son of Zerah, of the tribe of Judah, took of the accursed thing: and the anger of the Lord was kindled against the children of Israel.*

There are a lot more examples of God's anger in the Bible.[31] The point is that it is possible to get angry – and not sin[32]. The reality is that most of the time when we get <u>really</u> angry, we <u>really</u> sin. I believe that anger is something that almost everyone has a problem with from time to time. Most of us don't want to admit it. Anger can cause a multitude of sin. Obvious ones include lashing out with inappropriate language,

31   Deuteronomy 4:25; Judges 2:12; 2 Samuel 6:7; 1 Kings 14:15;
        1 Chronicles 13:10; Psalms 6:1
32   Ephesians 4:26

physical assault, and unacceptable gestures. Anger is also the culprit for more serious (in our eyes) sin, which can include everything from adultery to murder.

I still have a problem sometimes with my temper. I get mad and act in a way that I know I shouldn't. It is easy for me to say, "I don't care, I'm mad". The problem is that when we let our anger get the best of us, we do go mad. It is possible to lose control and act like a heathen. As a matter of fact, I am guessing that there are a whole lot of folks, including me, who would be very embarrassed if the rest of you could see us when we are throwing a little temper tantrum. Here's the problem. Every single time we talk about the subject of anger, we always quote the scripture that tells us to *"Be ye angry, and sin not"*. Then we say that it is OK to get mad, as long as you don't sin. Then we leave, go about our business, get angry, and sin.

How do we keep from allowing the emotion of anger - to cause us to sin? That is an easy question, with an easy answer. Unfortunately it is hard to accomplish – and it is impossible to accomplish without God. There are steps we have to take.

James 4: 7. *Submit yourselves therefore to God. Resist the devil, and he will flee from you.* **8.** *Draw nigh to God, and he will draw nigh to you. Cleanse your hands, ye sinners; and purify your hearts, ye double minded.*

The first thing we must do, and it is true of all sin in our life, is to submit ourselves to God. In the original language, the word "submit" means "to be subject to". In the case of anger this means that we let God respond to whatever it is that upsets us. As I said, this is not all that easy to do. The key is found in the way that the scripture is written. In order to successfully resist Satan, we can not wait 'till we are about to sin and then submit to God. We must seek God NOW. We have got to do our best to always and continually seek God. When we do that, it is a whole lot easier. It is easier, but it is still extremely difficult at times. So there is more.

Another step in fighting anger is to recognize that it is a problem, and vow that you are not going to allow it to defeat you. Anger causes hurt. It causes heartbreak. The damage that anger can inflict is awful. No one who is a slave to anger enjoys it. No rational person would ever proclaim, "You know, I really enjoy flying off of the handle and inflicting terror on my family". Look at scripture telling us about the fruit of the Spirit:

Galatians 5: 22. *But the fruit of the Spirit is love, joy, peace, longsuffering, gentleness, goodness, faith,* **23**. *Meekness, temperance: against such there is no law.*

Anger does not bring forth love, joy or peace. It is certainly not an indicator of longsuffering, gentleness, goodness or faith. A person who flys off of the handle is never meek. They are definitely not displaying temperance.

Proverbs 15 1. *A Soft answer turneth away wrath: but grievous words stir up anger.*

Whenever I am able to remember to put this into practice – it always works. When someone takes the initiative to act like a jerk, and they only get a response of politeness and kindness, it takes the wind right out of their sails. One thing is certain, if you respond to harsh words, with harsh words – things will escalate. The Bible says so:

Proverbs 15 18. **A** *wrathful man stirreth up strife: but he that is slow to anger appeaseth strife.*

I imagine that just about everyone has worked with or been around someone who was constantly stirring up trouble. A person like that makes things miserable in the workplace. They can destroy peace and harmony. On the other hand, it is a great addition to a team to have a person who never speaks ill of others, and who just does **not** get upset.

Proverbs 19: 11. *The discretion of a man deferreth his anger; and it is his glory to pass over a transgression.*

The literal translation for the word "*discretion*" is "intelligence or by implication, success". I don't know of anyone that has ever seen someone throw a little fit and said, "What an intelligent individual he is!"

Proverbs 31: 26. *She openeth her mouth with wisdom; and in her tongue is the law of kindness.*

This verse is addressing a mother and wife, but it speaks to everyone. There is a saying that "When mama's not happy, no one is happy". That is absolute truth, but the same is true for papa. We have an obligation as parents to not let our anger control us when we are dealing with our kids. We have the same obligation to our spouse. Unfortunately this is just about the hardest area of our lives in which to control anger.

BOTTOM LINE

Anger is not a sin. It does however put us on a very easy path that takes us through a very wide door that leads straight to a room that contains a plethora of sin. How do we avoid sinning when we are angry? We avoid it the same way we prepare for any battle. We train hard, and we make sure that we are wearing all of our armor when we enter the fight.

Ephesians 6: 12. *For we wrestle not against flesh and blood, but against principalities, against powers, against the rulers of the darkness of this world, against spiritual wickedness in high places.* **13**. *Wherefore take unto you the whole armour of God, that ye may be able to withstand in the evil day, and having done all, to stand.* **14.** *Stand therefore, having your loins girt about with* *truth, and having on the breastplate of righteousness;* **15.** *And your feet shod with the preparation of the gospel of peace;*

16. *Above all, taking the shield of faith, wherewith ye shall be able to quench all the fiery darts of the wicked.* **17.** *And take the helmet of salvation, and the sword of the Spirit, which is the word of God:* **18.** *Praying always with all prayer and supplication in the Spirit, and watching thereunto with all perseverance and supplication for all saints;*

Chapter Eight

Trouble in the (Church) Family

We celebrated our church anniversary not too long ago. Several folks gave testimonies which mentioned the church family. As they were speaking I agreed with them, and I could see heads in the congregation nodding in agreement. Our church family <u>is</u> important to us. Even so, we are still going to have problems with each other sometimes. Why? – because we are human. When we do have problems we've got two choices. We can bury our heads in the sand and say, "*No, we love each other too much. We will always agree. We will never fuss. There are no problems*" That is fairytale Christianity. I believe the second choice is more realistic. We can realize that we <u>will</u> disagree sometimes – and handle it like we try to handle everything else – scripturally. In order to do that, we have to be prepared. That is what this chapter is about.

I can't think of a better place to start than with Paul's writings to the church at Corinth. He addressed his letter to the <u>local church and to Christians</u>[33]. (That's us.) The first issue Paul addressed was division in the church. Take a look at the following scripture:

1 Corinthians 1: 10. *Now I beseech you, brethren, through the*

33   1 Corinthians 1:2

name of our Lord Jesus Christ, that ye all speak the same thing and that there be no divisions among you; but that ye be perfected together in the same mind and in the same judgment. **11.** *For it hath been signified unto me concerning you, my brethren, by them that are of the household of Chloe, that there are contentions among you.* **12.** *Now this I mean, that each one of you saith, I am of Paul; and I of Apollos: and I of Cephas; and I of Christ.* **13.** *Is Christ divided? was Paul crucified for you? or were ye baptized into the name of Paul?*

One of the things that always strikes me about verse eleven is that Paul flat tells on Chloe. He is saying to them, "Chloe's folks tell me that you guys are fighting." Then he starts to chew them out. I always wondered if Chloe got upset or embarrassed about this. I can just hear her saying, "Well for heaven's sake Paul, I didn't know you were going to tell them that **I** told you." Whether she minded or not, it didn't make much difference. Paul wrote these folks and gave them some instruction.

In verse ten he tells them that there should "*be no divisions among you*". Some people believe he is speaking of doctrinal differences. Others are convinced he is talking about personal squabbling. I think he means both. Why do I think that? I think that because he says **NO** divisions, and as far as I am concerned that is <u>exactly</u> what he meant. Let's take a peek at some of the types of division that can be found in a church.

1. **Power Struggles** – This seems to be what was plaguing the church at Corinth. There was a power struggle between the followers of Paul, Apollos, and Cephas. Paul tells them that it was Christ who was crucified for them, not him. I doubt if any one thing has split more churches than the issue of power (pride); People wanting to do things their way, disregarding the good of all, so they can have their way. They forget that Jesus is our foundation[34]. Every church, including

---

34   1 Corinthians 3:11

ours, has a set of "rules" for conducting daily business. (In our case it is our constitution and by-laws.) One of the obligations that all of us have when we are considering which church we will join, is to make a decision on whether or not we can live by them. Once we decide that we are OK with the way the business of the church is to be conducted, we have an obligation to abide by the rules, just like we would with any other organization.

NOTE: Nothing in this chapter should give anyone the idea that if something is not scripturally correct, we should keep quiet[35]. Certainly if any decision is being made, or if any action is being undertaken in a non-Biblical manner, we have an obligation to speak to our leaders. Even this can be, and should be done in a loving way. The second point is that there is always room for a dissenting opinion, again in a loving and respectful manner. As a matter of fact it is much less harmful to voice your opinion to your leadership, than it is to murmur your dissatisfaction to anyone who will listen. We can not always agree on every action taken. On a personal note – I have disagreed with several things my church has undertaken since I've been here. I have made my opinion known to the Pastor. He always listens, but if he disagrees he continues on course. When that happens it becomes my job to support his decision 100%. Side note: When we disagree – he is almost always right.

---

2. **Competition** – This is a kind of tough issue to address because as Americans we are very competitive. We always want to win. We always want to be the best. I don't know anyone who thinks there is anything wrong with competition. The problem comes when

---

that becomes our motivation for the work we do in the church. Every one of us is aware that we should serve because we love the Lord. We should serve because it is our privilege and our honor. If we are serving God so that we can receive the glory, we are wrong[36]. The Bible also addresses the issue of competition.

Philippians 2: 3 *doing nothing through faction or through vainglory, but in lowliness of mind each counting other better than himself;*

The Greek word for "*faction*" is (Strong's Ref. # 2052), "*eritheia*". Although the King James translators chose to translate it into "*faction*" it is just as accurate to use the word "*rivalry*". What is wrong with having rivalry as a motive for our service in the church? The main reason is because that violates our instruction from scripture. It is not difficult to understand why. If we start competing, there will soon be feelings hurt. When feelings get hurt, anger is next. It is easy to figure out what will eventually happen. Again – everything has to be taken in the context in which it is meant. For example, there is nothing wrong with kids having contests to see who can bring the most visitors.

The truth of the matter is that anything at all that we accomplish for the Lord, is for His glory, not for ours. Any success we have is because He has given us the wisdom and the circumstances to be successful. One of my most consistent prayers is that we NEVER forget that our church is doing well ONLY because we do everything only after much prayer, and because we are being led by the Holy Spirit.

3. **Silly Arguments** – There are lots of reasons we might get in personal arguments with each other. Some of the more unpleasant folks in the church I attend, make

36   1 Corinthians 1:31; 1 Corinthians 2:1-5; 1 Corinthians 10:31

people mad sometimes. It just happens. What about the rest of us who are so pleasingly pleasant? <u>Even</u> we are going to find someone is upset with us sometime in the next fifty years or so. It is amazing how angry Christians can get when they disagree. Understand what I'm talking about here. I'm not saying that we should not get angry – <u>ever</u>. We know that the Lord got/gets angry[37]. We know that there are times we should be angry, but in every case be careful not to let it cause us to sin[38]. Still, we can get silly sometimes. Look at what Paul says about this:

1 Corinthians 11:16 *But if any man seem to be contentious, we have no such custom, neither the churches of God.*

In the scriptures before verse sixteen Paul had just given a list of rules pertaining to head coverings in church. Verse sixteen says don't get silly and argue about it. One thing that burns me up is when a disagreement on scripture gets elevated to an importance that it does not deserve. You can get as adamant as you want when you are discussing the fact that Jesus   was resurrected after three days. Don't stay in a church that does not accept those types of facts. But – we should not allow ourselves to get sucked into silly, meaningless arguments about obscure passages that do not affect our core beliefs.

NOTE: I had to put this note in for all of you trouble makers who are thinking, "Zumwalt has gone too far this time. What does he mean calling some passages obscure and telling us they don't matter?" **Clarification**: Every word of every verse in the Bible is there for a reason – and matters. The more I study the more I am convinced of

---

37   Deuteronomy 1:37; 1 Kings 11:9; Psalms 7:11; Ecclesiastes 5:6;

38   Ephesians 4:26

that. And it is fun (and interesting) sometimes to engage in sincere discussion to determine what some of the more difficult passages might be saying. These types of passages however should never rise to the level of causing dissension among our church fellowship.

~~What are some of the things that we can do to keep from~~ falling into the traps that cause problems among church family members?

1 Corinthians 12: 26 *And whether one member suffer, all the members suffer with it; or one member be honoured, all the members rejoice with it.*

I've got to tell you, verse twenty-six describes something that my local church family does well. It is amazing how folks in our congregation gather round someone who needs help. This is true even for folks that we don't know well. Everyone in our church has a friend or two that they prefer to hang out with, to sit with, or just to carry on a conversation with. There are others in the church who we may not know quite as well. That is true because we are humans and we naturally gravitate towards certain types of people. All of this flies out the window when someone needs help. I am amazed every time we have a need in this church, to see the way that folks respond. I also believe that the same is true for when "*one member be honoured, all the members rejoice with it*".

Philippians 2:3 *Let nothing be done through strife or vainglory; but in lowliness of mind let each esteem other better than themselves.*

I had to put this verse in again one more time. This really is the key. If we all have the (true) heart of a servant, and have the correct motivation for coming to church and for serving the Lord, we will have no internal strife[39].

The Bible also contains instructions pertaining to fellow Christians who have completely left any walk they had with the Lord.

1 Corinthians 5: 11. *But now I have written unto you not to keep company, if any man that is called a brother be a fornicator, or covetous, or an idolater, or a railer, or a drunkard, or an extortioner; with such an one no not to eat.* **12.** *For what have I to do to judge them also that are without? do not ye judge them that are within?* **13.** *But them that are without God judgeth. Therefore put away from among yourselves that wicked person.*

2 Thessalonians 3:6 *Now we command you, brethren, in the name of our Lord Jesus Christ, that ye withdraw yourselves from every brother that walketh disorderly, and not after the tradition which he received of us.*

This is one of the areas of Christianity that it is easy to get in trouble with if you are not careful. Don't misunderstand me; I think the Bible is very clear. We are to avoid keeping company with certain types of individuals…who are Christians. Don't confuse these scriptures and think that Paul is telling us to avoid hanging around with sinners. If we didn't hang out with sinners, who would be left? These scriptures are alerting us to avoid Christians who are un-repentant and who continue in their sin. It is not an all inclusive list. There are lots of things that could be added (murderer, child molester, etc.). It is also not an all exclusive list. What do I mean by that?

I'll pick one category, "*drunkard*". We are not admonished to avoid contact with any Christian who has ever been a drunkard. If we were to get a list of sins that would cause us to avoid people forever – we could not go to dinner with anyone. It is my belief that we are being told that we should do nothing to condone the types of sins that these Christian folks are committing. If we continue in a relationship with a man, that knows that we know, that he is cheating on his wife, we are in essence condoning it. We are in a sense, communicating to him that we do not think that what he is doing is bad enough to warrant us changing our relationship with him. As we've discussed in our Sunday school class many times, there are scriptural consequences for our actions. If we are going to choose to live in unrepentant sin we better be prepared to face those consequences. Remember – these rules were written by God.

BOTTOM LINE

Being a church family member has rights, but it also has responsibilities. In our church family, as in our birth family, things can be a little tense sometimes. We must put our own feelings aside and remember that our responsibility is to the Lord. And above all – we must realize that we should always turn to the Bible for our instruction.

Hebrews 4: 12. *For the word of God is quick, and powerful, and sharper than any twoedged sword, piercing even to the dividing asunder of soul and spirit, and of the joints and marrow, and is a discerner of the thoughts and intents of the heart.*

Chapter Nine

Signs of False Teachers (& Preachers)

New Age creeping in to Churches

We've spent some time in our Sunday school class talking about false teachings. It is no secret that I am not a fan of some of the television preachers that are popular today. There are many that I believe are doing a wonderful job teaching the word of God. My problem is with all of the ones out there who are teaching and preaching false doctrine - and there are a lot of them. I feel the same about all the false teachers and preachers who are creeping into local churches around the nation. This is a very real problem that is with us right now. In this chapter we are going to take a look at what the Bible has to say about the subject of false religious teachings. What makes us think there are false teachers?

2 Peter 2:1 *But there were false prophets also among the people, even as there shall be false teachers among you, who privily shall bring in damnable heresies, even denying the Lord that bought them, and bring upon themselves swift destruction.*

At first glance this verse might cause us to ask "So what? The

Bible says that they will bring '*swift destruction*' upon themselves. If they deny '*the Lord that bought them*' who can they fool anyway?" Let's take a look at two men that this verse describes:

False Prophet	*Teachings*	*Problem*
Muhammad	Teaches that there is only one god – and he has no son. This is contrary to the Word of God – and by the way – was introduced in spite of Old Testament scripture available to Muhammad.	This is not the God of Christianity.
Joseph Smith	God gave Joseph Smith some added scriptures. Read **Revelation 22:18** and try to justify that. You can believe the Bible – or – the Book of Mormon but you can't believe both.	There is no profession of faith in Jesus Christ required – as the only way to heaven.

A lot of readers will be offended when I say Satan used these two men. Really good men and women are converting to Islam and to Mormonism every day. They believe they have found the truth because they have been fooled by these two <u>false</u> prophets. Listen, we have great men of God today that we admire. Some of the ones that come to mind are Billy Graham, Charles Stanley, David Jeremiah, our own Pastors, and the list goes on and on. Don't forget, **there are also great men who have been used by Satan.** Muhammad and Joseph Smith are two of the greatest.[40] I am even willing to concede that they might not have even been aware they were being used, that's how clever the enemy is.

If you have met many Mormons you know they are good and honest people. They are also sincere. I can imagine saying "thanks for helping me perpetrate this great hoax on all of the good people who might have become Christians if it were not for your help".

You might be saying, "that's all well and good, but there is no way that we have to worry about that kind of thing happening to us". Think again. I know that my local church *(Seven Lakes Baptist Church)* is a church based on scripture, led by Godly men who are guided by the Holy Spirit after much prayer and Bible study. As long as we continue this, our church will be blessed. Pastor Ken would always be the first to tell us, "Do not let your guard down". Why would our Pastor give us such a warning? Because he knows that churches all over this nation, and as a matter of fact some in the county I live in, are falling prey to this trap that Satan is so good at springing. But as always, don't take my word, look at the following verses:

Galatians2:4. *And that because of false brethren unawares brought in, who came in privily to spy out our liberty which we have in Christ Jesus, that they might bring us into bondage:*

Matthew 7:15 *Beware of false prophets, which come to you in <u>sheep's clothing,</u> but inwardly they are ravening wolves.*

40   That list also includes men like David Koresh and Jim Jones.

These verses perfectly point out the dangers we face today. So many churches are allowing new age doctrine to creep in. It starts out very slyly. Little by little customs, doctrines or ceremonies are introduced into the worship service; things that are not scriptural and are not of God. The Pastors of these churches, instead of standing up – allow them in the interest of keeping the peace. In many (yes many) cases this garbage continues until you have folks attempting to talk to the dead, predict the future, or figure out ways that you can get to heaven just by being good. The end product <u>is a church that teaches ways to get to heaven that are totally false</u>, in other words - ways other than a trust in Jesus Christ. When this happens – chalk up another huge win to Satan.

How does this happen? It can happen in a number of ways. The only limit on how Satan accomplishes this is his own imagination, and he is very good at what he does. One charismatic person can tear a church apart by teaching **<u>unchallenged</u>** false doctrine. Before you know what has happened, this person has a group of people following them that care more about him or her than they do about seeking the Gospel.

How do you keep this from happening to your church? Someday, some of us will, for one reason or another have to move. When we do we will have to look for another church. What should we look for? What should we look for even after we join another Bible teaching church? What should we do to protect the church we attend now?

1 Thessalonians 5:21 *Prove all things; hold fast that which is good.*

This should be the anchor verse for us. Obviously this verse is telling us to make sure that <u>anything</u>, that <u>anyone</u> tells us, teaches us or preaches to us is of God. How do we do that? We do it by looking at scripture and making certain. If someone tells you that God has a plan so that all really good people will end up in heaven someday, even though they refused to accept Jesus, they are telling you a lie. How do we know? We know because that is not what the Bible tells us. The reason these false teachers get away with this is because it is something that we would love to believe. The devil is excellent at finding lies that humans want to believe.

IF A MAN PERFORMS MIRACLES TODAY – DOESN'T HE HAVE TO BE GODLY?

Acts 8:9. *But there was a certain man, called Simon, which beforetime in the same city used sorcery, and bewitched the people of Samaria, giving out that himself was some great one:* **10.** *To whom they all gave heed, from the least to the greatest, saying, This man is the great power of God.* **11.** *And to him they had regard, because that of long time he had bewitched them with sorceries.* **12.** *But when they believed Philip preaching the things concerning the kingdom of God, and the name of Jesus Christ, they were baptized, both men and women.* **13.** *Then Simon himself believed also: and when he was baptized, he continued with Philip, and wondered, beholding the miracles and signs which were done.*

THIS IS NOT CORRECT: Simon was fooling people. He made them believe that he was of God because he could seemingly perform all kinds of miracles. There was one guy who knew for sure that Simon was not a Godly man – Simon himself. When Simon heard the true gospel he wanted that power. There are several significant points here that relate to our lesson. One is that when Simon was "bewitching them with sorceries" he <u>never</u> proclaimed God. Who did the people give regard to? They gave it to <u>Simon</u>, because of what <u>he</u> was able to do. The second point is that even Simon, who was full of the devil, was able to get saved. Never – ever give up on anyone when you are seeking his or her salvation. Another point here is that we have "Simons" everywhere. This passage of scripture points out how easily we can be fooled. Even if he is preaching the Word of God – Don't turn to the man – turn to the Word. That is what happened in Samaria.

How do we know that the fortunetellers today have not been given a special power by God?

Micah 5:10. *And it shall come to pass in that day, saith the Lord, that I will cut off thy horses out of the midst of thee, and I will destroy thy chariots:* **11**. *And I will cut off the cities of thy land, and throw down all thy strong holds:* **12**. *And I will cut off witchcrafts out of thine hand; and thou shalt have no more soothsayers:*

Does that sound like God is happy with fortunetellers and people who claim witch powers? Does it sound like God is going to help or bless them? The verse does not say, "except for the ones who I have given power to". The fact that **all** of them will be cut off is extremely clear. It is not possible to read any other meaning into this.

HOW DO WE KNOW WHAT IS OF GOD?

1 John 4: 1 *Beloved, believe not every spirit, but try the spirits whether they are of God: because many false prophets are gone out into the world.* **2.** *Hereby know ye the Spirit of God: Every spirit that confesseth that Jesus Christ is come in the flesh is of God:* **3** *And every spirit that confesseth not that Jesus Christ is come in the flesh is not of God: and this is that spirit of antichrist, whereof ye have heard that it should come; and even now already is it in the world.*

This is a very important passage. I think it is often misunderstood. Do not be fooled into thinking that just

because someone can proclaim that Christ is the Son of God that they are <u>of</u> God.

James 2:19 *Thou believest that there is one God; thou doest well: the devils also believe, and tremble.*

If you met a person on the street and they told you they were a Doctor you wouldn't just take their word for it and allow them to operate on you. You would want some proof. You'd make a visit to their office, take a look at the surroundings, get comfortable with them, and check out their credentials. Take a minute and relate this same amount of care to someone who claims to be of God. Just because they tell you that they believe in God and Jesus, don't be fooled into thinking that is enough. They have got to be willing to <u>proclaim</u> the full and unedited version of the Gospel. The minute they start drifting off into other areas – drop them. Even ***"the devils also believe and tremble"***.

> **Note:** Here we go again with that line we talk about sometimes. We are talking about false teachers and false doctrine. We are <u>not</u> talking about disagreements in <u>every case</u>. We know there are some things we <u>can not disagree on</u>. The plan of salvation, virgin birth, etc. are examples. There are however, some things that we might not agree on – but that should not cause chaos or disruption in our Church. For example, most of us believe that Paul's affliction was his bad eyesight. You might think he was hard of hearing. We can discuss it, talk about it and even continue to disagree on it. We can live with these disagreements. These types of issues are <u>not</u> what this chapter is about. The line here is actually very clear, although Satan is good at blurring it sometimes.

WHAT ABOUT *MY* EXPERIENCE?

There are many good people who will tell you that they have had a visit from their dead uncle or someone else they were close to. They will tell you that the person was sent to them by God to help them in some way. There are an equal number of folks who will tell you that they had a personal visit from God, Jesus or an angel. These people will tell you, *"I don't care what the Bible says, I know what I saw and what I heard"*. How do we respond to these folks?

Exodus 7:10 *And Moses and Aaron went in unto Pharaoh, and they did so as the Lord had commanded: and Aaron cast down his rod before Pharaoh, and before his servants, and it became a serpent.* *12* *Then Pharaoh also called the wise men and the sorcerers: now the magicians of Egypt, they also did in like manner with their enchantments.*

When Aaron (not Moses by the way) cast his rod down God turned it into a serpent Pharaoh said, "big deal, watch this". He called his flunkeys in to duplicate this - and obviously Satan helped them. They were able to do the same thing. Moses and Aaron could have said, "Whoa, I guess their god is equal to our God" and then left. They didn't do that. They stayed and allowed God to show Pharaoh that He could overcome anything that Satan could do. In today's world, people are eager to believe anything Satan lays before them. Any appearance of a miracle and some folks are ready to throw the scriptures aside and trust their eyes, <u>completely forgetting their faith</u>.

1 Peter 1:5 *Who are kept by the power of God through faith unto salvation ready to be revealed in the last time.* *8.* *Whom having not seen, ye love; in whom, though now ye see him not, yet believing, ye rejoice with joy unspeakable and full of glory:* *9.* *Receiving the end of your faith, even the salvation of your souls.*

Ephesians 6:16 *Above all, taking the shield of faith, wherewith ye shall be able to quench all the fiery darts of the wicked.*

Is God sending you a sign? Is it possible God is giving you a sign so that you'll know once and for all He is God. What if you prayed and asked Him for a sign?

Mark 8:11. *And the Pharisees came forth, and began to question with him, seeking of him a sign from heaven, tempting him.* **12**. *And he sighed deeply in his spirit, and saith, Why doth this generation seek after a sign? verily I say unto you, There shall no sign be given unto this generation.*

Is this clear enough? "There shall be no sign" is hard to mistake. What would make us think that God would make an exception for us? God and Angels appeared in the Old Testament – why not now? You might ask, how do you know that God doesn't pop in from time to time and instruct some people personally? After all, God or His angels appeared to people all the time in the Old (and New) Testament. I would not presume to tell you that God would never – under any circumstances send a visible angel to someone. There are lots of stories by Godly persons that make us wonder. I would only strongly caution you to be very careful with it. God has given us the wonderful gift of the <u>Holy Spirit, and the Bible and prayer</u>. That is the way God communicates with us today.

Ephesians 3:5 *Which in other ages was not made known unto the sons of men, as it is now revealed unto his holy apostles and prophets by the Spirit;*

Ephesians 6:17 *And take the helmet of salvation, and the sword of the Spirit, which is the word of God:*

John 15:26 *But when the Comforter is come, whom I will* *send unto you from the Father, even the Spirit of truth, which proceedeth from the Father, he shall testify of me:*

John 16: 12. *I have yet many things to say unto you, but ye cannot bear them now. **13**. Howbeit when he, the Spirit of truth, is come, he will guide you into all truth: for he shall not speak of himself; but whatsoever he shall hear, that shall he speak: and he will shew you things to come.*

1 John 2: 27 *But the anointing which ye have received of him abideth in you, and ye need not that any man teach you: but as the same anointing teacheth you of all things, and is truth, and is no lie, and even as it hath taught you, ye shall abide in him.*

Romans 8: 9 *But ye are not in the flesh, but in the Spirit, if so be that the Spirit of God dwell in you. Now if any man have not the Spirit of Christ, he is none of his. **10**. And if Christ be in you, the body is dead because of sin; but the Spirit is life because of righteousness. **11**. But if the Spirit of him that raised up Jesus from the dead dwell in you, he that raised up Christ from the dead shall also quicken your mortal bodies by his Spirit that dwelleth in you.*

Romans 8:16 *The Spirit itself beareth witness with our spirit, that we are the children of God:*

1 Corinthians 2:10 *But God hath revealed them unto us by his Spirit: for the Spirit searcheth all things, yea, the deep things of God.*

Matthew 2:12 *Now we have received, not the spirit of the world, but the spirit which is of God; that we might know the things that are freely given to us of God. **13**. Which things also we speak, not in the words which man's wisdom teacheth, but which the Holy Ghost teacheth; comparing spiritual things with spiritual **14** But the natural man receiveth not the things of the Spirit of God: for* *they are foolishness unto him: neither can he know them, because they are spiritually discerned.*

1 Corinthians 3:16 *Know ye not that ye are the temple of God, and that the Spirit of God dwelleth in you?*

Ephesians 1:17 *That the God of our Lord Jesus Christ, the Father of glory, may give unto you the spirit of wisdom and revelation in the knowledge of him:* **18**. *The eyes of your understanding being enlightened; that ye may know what is the hope of his calling, and what the riches of the glory of his inheritance in the saints,*

Galations 3:14 *That the blessing of Abraham might come on the Gentiles through Jesus Christ; that we might receive the promise of the Spirit through faith.*

Galations 3:5 *He therefore that ministereth to you the Spirit, and worketh miracles among you, doeth he it by the works of the law, or by the hearing of faith?*

WHAT DO YOU SAY TO SOMEONE WHO IS FOOLED BY A DAVID KORESH INTO BELIEVING THEY ARE JESUS? WELL, YOU SHOULD QUOTE SCRIPTURE TO THEM:

Matthew 24:4 *And Jesus answered and said unto them, Take heed that no man deceive you.* **5**. *For many shall come in my name, saying, I am Christ; and shall deceive many.*

6. *And ye shall hear of wars and rumours of wars: see that ye be not troubled: for all these things must come to pass, but the end is not yet.* **7**. *For nation shall rise against nation, and kingdom against kingdom: and there shall be famines, and pestilences, and* *earthquakes, in divers places.* **8.** *All these are the beginning of sorrows.*

9. *Then shall they deliver you up to be afflicted, and shall kill you: and ye shall be hated of all nations for my name's sake.* **10.** *And then shall many be offended, and shall betray one another, and shall hate one another.* **11.** *And many false prophets shall rise, and shall deceive many.*

Matthew 24: 23. *Then if any man shall say unto you, Lo, here is Christ, or there; believe it not.* **24.** *For there shall arise false Christs, and false prophets, and shall shew great signs and wonders; insomuch that, if it were possible, they shall deceive the very elect.*

25. *Behold, I have told you before.* **26.** *Wherefore if they shall say unto you, Behold, he is in the desert; go not forth: behold, he is in the secret chambers; believe it not.* **27.** *For as the lightning cometh out of the east, and shineth even unto the west; so shall also the coming of the Son of man be.*

Mark 13: 22. *For false Christs and false prophets shall rise, and shall shew signs and wonders, to seduce, if it were possible, even the elect.*

That's what you say to them. You show them the Bible. They might ask you, "But what if the guy can perform miracles? What if he is everything that I ever believed Jesus was? What if he has a holy countenance and physical attributes that appear to be heavenly?" Take a look at the following verses. They speak for themselves.

2 Corinthians 11:13. *For such are false apostles, deceitful workers, transforming themselves into the apostles of Christ.* **14.** *And no marvel; for Satan himself is transformed into an angel of light.* **15.** *Therefore it is no great thing if his ministers also be* *transformed as the ministers of righteousness; whose end shall be according to their works.*

2 Corinthians 11:26. *In journeyings often, in perils of waters, in perils of robbers, in perils by mine own countrymen, in perils by the heathen, in perils in the city, in perils in the wilderness, in perils in the sea, in perils among false brethren;*

I wanted to re-visit this passage because of what Paul is saying here. Paul has been through every danger imaginable. When he lists the dangers he has seen he lists false brethren right along with his shipwrecks, being robbed, thrown in jail and beaten, and almost drowning. Most of us will never face the dangers Paul faced… except that is for false brethren. The good news is that all we have to do is be vigilant in the Word.

Galatians2:4. *And that because of false brethren unawares brought in, who came in privily to spy out our liberty which we have in Christ Jesus, that they might bring us into bondage:*

This verse is significant because it says, "false brethren <u>brought</u> in". In other words these guys didn't just fall out of a station wagon in front of the church and wander inside – they were brought in for a specific reason. Who brought them in? Satan, of course.

BOTTOM LINE

It is a terrible thing for a church to find itself in the middle of a feud. Christians should seek to work together prayerfully, led by men of God who pray daily and are guided by scripture and the Holy Spirit. Those of us who depend on these Godly men for guidance have an obligation to be good followers, doing what we can to implement the plans that our Pastor and Deacons have for the future of our Church.

We have another obligation to these men. We have an obligation to help them keep our local church wholly in the will of God. We do this by praying and reading <u>and </u>studying the Bible. We do this by knowing false teachings when we hear them. There is always a danger of someone not fully understanding this and insisting that we agree on every little detail. We **<u>will</u>** all agree – when we get to heaven. As long as we are human we're gonna look at things a little differently than the next person does, and that's OK. There is a line that we can cross. Do not let Satan blur that line.

Chapter Ten

A Realistic Look at Bible Stories

I wanted to do something a little different in this chapter. I wanted to take a look at some of the stories we grew up with, from a little different vantage point. I want us to try to place ourselves in the shoes of the persons who actually lived through some of these events. The reason I wanted to do this was to get a more down-to-earth appreciation of what they went through. I figured that a good way to do this would be to look at the life of Jesus.

LUKE 1:26-38

We've heard the Christmas story a thousand times, but I'm curious if we've ever stopped to really consider how the folks involved felt. Imagine Mary, the mother of Jesus. The Bible does not tell how old she was at the time of His birth. My belief is that she was somewhere in the neighborhood of sixteen years old. I arrived at that conclusion from reading about that period of time and that part of the world. I am not prepared to argue, so if you believe she was older (or younger) I have no problem with that. The fact remains that she was very young.

Obviously Mary was a incredibly devout young lady, and a virgin. This un-married young woman has a visit from the angel Gabriel. Gabriel informs her that she is about to "*conceive in thy womb, and bring forth a son*". Put yourself in her shoes for a few minutes. In the time and the place that Mary lived, rules involving morality were incredibly strict. A female could be put to death by stoning for having a sexual relationship outside of marriage. At the very least Mary had to think of what it would be like to have to inform her parents. She had to wonder what Joseph was going to say. Although we have made it into a cute little Christmas story, Mary was in a compromising situation. It took a lot of courage for her to tell Gabriel, "*Behold the handmaid of the Lord; be it unto me according to thy word*".

Some of the questions that come to my mind are:

1. What do you think her parents said? I wonder how they treated her.
2. The Bible tells us that Joseph was "*was minded to put her away privily*".[41] After the "*angel of the Lord appeared unto him in a dream*" he changed his mind. What do you think the scene was like between Joseph and Mary when she informed him she was going to have a baby? Do you think Joseph was furious and yelled at her? Do you think he was so hurt that he could not talk about it? Even today it is a huge disgrace in that part of the world for an un-married woman to become pregnant, and Joseph's fiancé was about to have a baby that he <u>knew</u> was not his.
3. I wonder how the people in the town treated Mary. Did they treat her as an outcast? Did the men make fun of Joseph and accuse him of being a fool? Did the women in the town say hurtful things to Mary's parents?

---

41   Matthew 1:19-25

LUKE 2:1-7

The next part of the story I want to look at is the actual birth of Jesus. Joseph and Mary had to travel to from Nazareth to the city of Bethlehem for tax purposes. The Governor was Cyrenius. He required everyone to travel back to the land they were from and be counted. That meant that Joseph, along with a very pregnant Mary had to make the trip. Depending on the route that they took they had to travel between sixty and seventy-five miles. No matter what their method of travel, it could not have been easy for Mary.

If a person walks four miles an hour, they are walking a pretty brisk pace. There is no way that Mary and Joseph could have maintained a pace like that. Not only was Mary about to deliver, but they also had to have quite a few provisions for such a long trip. Counting stops to eat, bathroom breaks (which every mom and dad knows that Mary needed a lot of), the terrain they were negotiating, two - three miles per hour would probably be about their average pace. If they traveled for ten hours a day it would have taken two to three days to arrive. Can you imagine how worn out Mary must have been?

Once Mindi and I were on vacation with the kids and were driving home. We were somewhere near Indianapolis. We were worn out from driving and decided to stop for the night. What we did not know was the **Brickyard 500** was being run the next day. We had to drive another 75 miles before we could find a motel that had a vacancy. We were **driving** and we were miserable.

Not only were Mary and Joseph walking – but – they did not have the traditional motels like we think of today. There were inns, but not the type that we imagine. Tradition called for you to stay with your family. During the tax time that meant that all of the rooms in the house would be shared by arriving relatives. As if that wasn't bad enough, Mary needed some privacy in order to give birth. The Bible says "*there was no room for them in the inn*". I would be surprised if there was more than one Inn in Bethlehem. They were hard pressed for a place to stay if they settled for a manger.

I want to throw in a brief description of the kind of city they entered. It was over crowded and full of strangers. There were dangers from thieves and the Jews always had to be fearful of the Roman soldiers. Even in the year 2003 many small villages in various parts of the world are without proper plumbing, which is something that we take for granted. There were animals everywhere, which meant there was animal waste everywhere. In other words, it was not a pleasant place to be – at all. To make matters even worse, Joseph and Mary ended up in the worst possible place they could have landed, a manger. I doubt if there is anyone who has not been to a barn where cattle or horses were kept. You know that you can smell it a long ways off. You also know that no matter how clean they might be, you would not want to give birth in one. (I wouldn't even want to eat a sandwich in one.) I imagine that Joseph tried to get some fresh hay to make a spot that was clean for Mary. Still, compared to the sterile, highly supervised births that we are used to in a modern hospital, the conditions that our Savior was born in were horrendous. Why do you think that God chose to have His Son born this way? What do you think that Mary and Joseph thought about this?

Note: There is one thing I want us to keep in mind as we discuss this. Everyone believed that when the Christ arrived, He would come in a blaze of glory. They believed He would rise up and free the Jews from the tyranny that they suffered under. Most Jews believed that the Savior would be a mighty warrior who would organize them and lead them into battle to drive out their oppressors. I can't help but believe that Mary and Joseph had to wonder what was going on – the King of the Jews born in a manger?

Luke 2:8-20

Here we have the story of the Shepherds in the field with their sheep. No doubt these fellows were familiar with the scriptures which prophesied the coming of Jesus. I wonder if they had carried on conversations like we do today. I wonder if they said "You know, this could be the day that the Messiah comes", kind of like we say, "You know, this could be the day the Lord returns". They probably didn't think so anymore than we do when we say it.

Shepherds in that part of the world are a pretty tough looking group of men. They are all alone, pretty much in the middle of nowhere. Their duty is to take care of their flock, which includes guarding them from predators. I doubt if there is much these guys were afraid of. The scripture tells us that when the angel appeared these guys *"were sore afraid"*, and I don't blame them. The angel told them *"Fear not: for, behold, I bring you good tidings of great joy"*. There is no way these guys could possibly have realized just how good the tidings were, or how great the joy would be.

After the angel told them where they could find Jesus, a whole host appeared in the sky and began to sing praises to God. What must these shepherds have thought? There was no way they would not go to the manger to see the baby Jesus. When they got there they *"made known abroad the saying which was told them concerning this child."* In other words they told Mary and Joseph what they had seen and heard. This had to be a great comfort to the parents. I love the scripture that says *"But Mary kept all these things, and pondered them in her heart*[42]*."* The reason I like that verse is because I believe it must have been a comfort to Mary in helping her to prepare for some of the things that she would have to endure.

I can't help but wonder what the shepherds thought when they saw Jesus in the filthy conditions He was born into. Did they wonder how in the world this child could grow up and save them from Rome? Were they so amazed by the appearance

[42]   Verse 19

of the angels that they were not capable of doubting? Did they spend the rest of their lives telling people the story of what had happened to them, and did people believe them? We do know that *"the shepherds returned, glorifying and praising God for all the things that they had heard and seen, as it was told unto them."* I have lots of questions about the shepherds – and about the wise men. I'm gonna ask them someday.

MATTHEW 2: 1-12

Mary and Joseph were still in Bethlehem. There are scholars who believe that they did not return to Nazareth because there were those who would not accept the virgin birth, and would have made life miserable for the very young couple. No matter the reason, they were still in Bethlehem when the wise men from the east arrived. Can you imagine what a shock this must have been? Tradition places the number of wise men at three, probably because they bought three gifts, *"gold, and frankincense[43], and myrrh[44]"*. The more I read about this the more I think that the number was much greater. Here is how I arrived at this **opinion**:

The gifts that these fellows bought were very expensive. There is no record of the quantity of each that they gave. From reading about the times and the types of persons who would have been likely to have traveled such a great distance to see Jesus, it seems likely to me that they would not have made

---

[43]   An odorous resin imported from Arabia (Isa. 60:6; Jer. 6:20), yet also growing in Palestine (Cant. 4:14). It was one of the ingredients in the perfume of the sanctuary (Ex. 30:34), and was used as an accompaniment of the meat-offering (Lev. 2:1, 16; 6:15; 24:7). When burnt it emitted a fragrant odor, and hence the incense became a symbol of the Divine name (Mal. 1:11; Cant. 1:3) and an emblem of prayer (Ps. 141:2; Luke 1:10; Rev. 5:8; 8:3).

[44]   A gum resin, usually of a yellowish brown or amber color, of an aromatic odor, and a bitter, slightly pungent taste. It is valued for its odor and for its medicinal properties.

the trip alone. I think there is a good possibility that they would have had a number of servants with them. The make-up of their group could probably have qualified as a caravan. Imagine what these two very young parents must have thought when the magi arrived at their house and presented their infant son with such expensive gifts.

I wonder what kinds of conversations that Mary and Joseph had with each other when these fellows left. They had to wonder who else might show up. Did they discuss what to do with the gifts? You'd think that by this time they would not do anything at all without praying about it first. Put yourself in their shoes and imagine a group of rich guys showing up and wanting to worship <u>your</u> child, and then leaving you some very expensive gifts. When these fellas left, they went a different way so that Herod would not find out where Jesus was. About the same time Joseph was warned in a dream to flee to Egypt.

Matthew 2: 13-18

Depending on the route that Joseph took, and where he settled, it was over two hundred miles to Egypt at best. It could not have been a pleasant journey. Besides the fact that it is barren waste land, they had more to worry about than the usual. They had to be thinking about the danger of meeting Roman soldiers on the road who might question them and kill their child. Do you think that their faith was so great by now that they were not a bit worried? Or do you think that as humans we never seem to reach that stage, no matter how much we are reassured?

There is another point here that I want us to think about; the absolute cruelty that existed in that day. Herod ordered soldiers to kill every male child, two years old and younger. If our President ordered soldiers to travel to a certain area in our country and kill children, he would immediately be driven out of office. On top of that, soldiers would refuse to carry out such an order. Imagine the cruelty of killing children? Pulling the child from the arms of a screaming mother and slaying him by sword almost defies our ability to imagine, but that is exactly what happened. That is the type of tyranny that the Jews were counting on Jesus to free them from. That helps to understand why so many Jews were disappointed when He arrived as a servant and not as a conquering hero.

One reason that I wanted to include this particular episode is because, when we really stop to think about what happened, we realize what horrors the Jewish citizens suffered and how much they were counting on the Messiah to save them.

LUKE 2:40

We don't know a whole lot about Jesus as a child. What do you think he was like? Did everyone like Him? Was He so good that some folks could not stand Him? Did anyone hate Him? Obviously He was a wonderful Son who never gave His parents any trouble, at least in the traditional sense. I wonder if any of His young friends ever looked at Him and thought, "Don't you <u>ever</u> do anything wrong?"

It would have been Mary's job to teach Jesus the scriptures. She was aware of the fact that He was born to be a King. I wonder how the learning process went for Jesus. Did He read something one time and then remember it? Did He just know scripture without having to be taught? When he helped His step dad Joseph in the carpenter shop, was Jesus a perfect carpenter? Was He a better carpenter than anyone else?

As I stated before, there is little known about Jesus as a child. We do get some insight into His life at age twelve.

LUKE 2: 41-49

Mary and Joseph were taking their family on the annual pilgrimage to Jerusalem for the Feast of the Passover. Jesus was twelve years old. When they were finished, they left to begin their journey back home. Jesus had never been a problem before. They could always count on Him to be where He was supposed to be, when He was supposed to be there. It is no surprise that they figured He was somewhere with family, on the journey home. I doubt if it would have ever occurred to them that Jesus would have stayed behind when they left.

After a full days travel they missed Him. I always figured that when they stopped for the night they realized that Jesus was missing. If I had been Joseph I would have been terrified, wondering where my son could be. They traveled back and searched for Him for three days. They finally found Him in the temple, *"sitting in the midst of the doctors, both hearing them, and asking them questions"*. This was a pretty amazing thing. In those days everyone had a certain place in the temple. There is no way in the world that a child of twelve would even be allowed to speak, much less be allowed to question a group of elders. Jesus was so full of knowledge, and so wise, that He captivated this group. The Bible tells us *"all that heard him were astonished at his understanding and answers"*. If they were astonished at His answers, they must have been asking Him questions.

NOTE: To understand how amazing this scene is, you have to have an understanding of the way the temple was run. No one could approach the Priest just because they wanted to. As a matter of fact, children had no status whatsoever in the temple. Even un-married men had to take a place in the back, and were not allowed to speak unless spoken to. For a group of "holy men" to place themselves in a subservient position to Jesus was absolutely unheard of. The only thing I can think of to compare it to would be if your twelve year old child disappeared in Washington D.C. and you found him surrounded by Senators who were asking him questions and taking notes. I don't know about you – but I'd be pretty surprised to find my son in that situation.

The Bible tells us in verse 51 that once again "*his mother kept all these sayings in her heart.*" Mary is the one person on earth who knew, beyond any shadow of a doubt that Jesus was indeed the Son of God, born of a virgin birth[45]. Even with that sure knowledge, I wonder if she was ever caught off guard. I wonder if she had the fear that any mother would have had when Jesus was missing; or did she have a calm assurance because of her knowledge? When they found Jesus He seemed to be aggravated with them. He asked, "*How is it that ye sought me? wist ye not that I must be about my Father's business46?*" It makes me think that even after all they had been through, Mary and Joseph still had a hard time realizing just how special Jesus really was.

MATTHEW 3: 1-17

John the Baptist has to be one of the most interesting guys in the Bible. He appeared to be a wild man, preaching in the wilderness. He dressed in camel skins and he ate locusts and wild honey. He had no money and I always pictured him looking like what we would consider a lunatic. He was anointed with the Holy Spirit, and had been since conception[47]. As a result of this anointing he was extremely effective in his task of announcing the coming of Jesus. I have been to the area where Jesus was baptized by John. To describe it as a wilderness is accurate. There is nothing pretty about the area. For John the Baptist to even survive in that vicinity is a miracle. The fact that anyone would come to hear him preach is even more amazing.

When John saw Jesus he recognized Him immediately as the Messiah[48]. There is no reason for us to believe that John the Baptist knew that his cousin Jesus was the Messiah before that

---

45   Luke 1:35
46   Luke 2:49
47   Luke 1:15
48   John 1:29

moment. There is every reason to believe that they knew each other before that day, and even that they might have played together as children[49]. The only answer I can think of is that the Lord chose that moment to reveal to John that Jesus was the one that John the Baptist was preaching about.

It is also interesting to me that John did not back down one bit from the Pharisees and Sadducees who came to see him. These guys must have hated John because so many people were coming to hear him preach. John was telling them that they could be forgiven of their sins without going through the Priest[50]. This was money out of their pocket. These were some powerful men but John the Baptist was without fear in the way he spoke to them[51]. These guys did not care what John preached and they did not care about the people that were there to hear him. All they cared about was the fact that they were losing money and power.

JOHN 2: 1-11

Up to now Jesus had performed no miracles. There was no reason for anyone who knew Him to suppose that He was capable of performing them. His first miracle was performed at a wedding where Jesus and His mother were guests. We all know the story. They ran out of wine and Mary asked Jesus to help. What made her think that He could/would? Had she seen Him perform miracles before that we know nothing about? Did she just know, because of who she knew Him to be that He was capable of solving this simple problem?

When Jesus had the servants fill the jugs with water and take them into the governor of the feast, I wonder what they were thinking. The governor had demanded wine, and they gave him water. Did they slink off to hide? Think about it for a minute. There was no reason for them to believe that when

---

49   Luke 1:36-42
50   Matthew 3:6
51   Matthew 3:7

the boss took a drink, he was not going to spit it out and yell, "This is water. Someone bring those idiot servants here so I can beat them in front of everyone for humiliating me like this." After he tasted the wine and announced how delicious that it was, I wonder what the servants thought then. Did they tell everyone they saw for the rest of their lives, and did anyone believe them?

MARK 1: 40-45

This is the story of Jesus healing a leper. I have done some reading on the subject of how lepers were treated in Jesus' time. They had to call out in a loud voice, "Unclean". This was to warn people to avoid them. They were required to avoid people and it was their responsibility to stay out of everyone else's way. They were allowed to go almost nowhere, and they survived by begging. Once a person was suspected of having leprosy they were quarantined by the Priest for ten days. At the end of that time if they were found to <u>not</u> have it, the Priest would announce it and the person could resume their place in society.

As the disease began to manifest itself the person began to literally rot away. They would lose chunks of tissue from various parts of their body, becoming a sickening mess. No one wanted them around. Not only did they look and smell hideous, they were very contagious and no one wanted to catch the disease. As if all of this was not bad enough it was believed (and taught by the Priests) that they were ill because of a great sin in their life. There were supposed to be eleven sins, that if committed would be punished by leprosy. (I don't know what they were.)

When this leper approached Jesus he was breaking the rules big time. He was not supposed to be anywhere near another person, much less approach them. When he approached Jesus, Jesus did an amazing thing. He reached out and touched this hideous wretch. Can you imagine the shock that must have gone through the crowd when Jesus did this? Imagine the shock when the man was healed. Jesus told the guy to keep his mouth shut, and to go see the Priest so that he could be declared fit for society. The fellow did what any of us would have done and told everyone of his good fortune. This caused such great commotion that Jesus was forced to leave the city and go to "*desert places*".

Bottom Line

This could go on forever. I've enjoyed this chapter – a lot. If you are thinking that there really has not been much of a point – you are right. I just wanted us to take time to realize the reality of the circumstances that some of the people in the Bible found themselves in. Sometimes I think we treat these stories too much like a *Fairy Tale*, and forget that they involved <u>real</u> people, who showed a tremendous amount of courage. I'm sure you noticed that I put my opinion in an awful lot. I don't normally do that, and I want to be sure that you realize that it is **JUST** my opinion. If it is not in scripture, be sure that you question it!

Chapter Eleven

The Bible – Are There Discrepancies?

As I try to figure out what we should do for Sunday school each week, I think about some of the classes that we've had. We've discussed dinosaur killers, the different interpretations of the Bible and the different commentaries on the Bible. The folks in the class do what they are supposed to do – they test <u>everything</u> with scripture. That is what led me to this (kind of strange) subject. What about the things in the Bible that are very clear, but do not seem to make sense? I've chosen an example that I used to wonder about when I was a little boy in Sunday school.

Matthew 4:18 *And Jesus, walking by the sea of Galilee, saw two brethren, Simon called Peter, and Andrew his brother, casting a net into the sea: for they were fishers.* **19.** *And he saith unto them, Follow me, and I will make you fishers of men.* **20.** *And they straightway left their nets, and followed him.* **21.** *And going on from thence, he saw other two brethren, James the son of Zebedee, and John his brother, in a ship with Zebedee their father, mending their nets; and he called them.* **22.** *And they immediately left the ship and their father, and followed him.*

When I learned this as a kid I wondered why in the world these guys would just quit their job, and go and follow Jesus. My teacher said he thought there were several reasons, but he was not exactly sure why either. I just figured they hated fishing so much they were glad for any excuse to get away. When I got older I studied my Bible on my own and figured out the reason. Look at the next passage of scripture:

Luke 5: 1. *And it came to pass, that, as the people pressed upon him to hear the word of God, he stood by the lake of Gennesaret,* **2.** *And saw two ships standing by the lake: but the fishermen were gone out of them, and were washing their nets.* **3.** *And he entered into one of the ships, which was Simon's, and prayed him that he would thrust out a little from the land. And he sat down, and taught the people out of the ship.* **4.** *Now when he had left speaking, he said unto Simon, Launch out into the deep, and let down your nets for a draught.* **5.** *And Simon answering said unto him, Master, we have toiled all the night, and have taken nothing: nevertheless at thy word I will let down the net.* **6.** *And when they had this done, they inclosed a great multitude of fishes: and their net brake.* **7.** *And they beckoned unto their partners, which were in the other ship, that they should come and help them. And they came, and filled both the ships, so that they began to sink.* **8.** *When Simon Peter saw it, he fell down at Jesus' knees, saying, Depart from me; for I am a sinful man, O Lord.* **9.** *For he was astonished, and all that were with him, at the draught of the fishes which they had taken:* **10.** *And so was also James, and John, the sons of Zebedee, which were partners with Simon. And Jesus said unto Simon, Fear not; from henceforth thou shalt catch men.* **11.** *And when they had brought their ships to land, they forsook all, and followed him.*

The scripture from Luke goes into a little more detail and explains to us that there was more to the story than we knew from reading the passage in Matthew. Jesus taught these fishermen, no doubt impressing them quite a bit with His manner and His knowledge. On top of that, they figured He had to be special because He showed them how to catch enough fish to tear their nets and almost sink their boats. Although it explains why they were so eager to follow Jesus, it presents another problem. These two scriptures seem to contradict each other. I've listed the contradictions:

Matthew	**Luke**
Took place on the Sea of Galilee	*Took place on the Lake of Gennesaret*
Jesus saw two brothers, Simon Peter and Andrew / **Then** "*going on from* thence" *He saw two other brothers* ", James the son of Zebedee, and John his brother".	*Jesus had them take their boats out and after He taught them, He instructed them to do a little fishing. After they caught all of the fish, they landed their boats and THEN they followed Him. It sounds like (from verse 11) that they all took off and followed Him at the same time.*

Before we discuss these apparent contradictions, I want to look at the definition of the word "contradiction". This is what Webster[52] says:

Contradiction: *Something containing contradictory elements.*

Contradictory: *Either of two propositions related in such a way that it is impossible for both to be true or both to be false.*

Let's apply that test to the above scripture. How can we possibly explain the first apparent inconsistency? The first thing we do is to fall back on our faith and realize that there <u>is</u>

---

52   *Webster's II New Riverside University Dictionary*, Boston, MA: The Riverside Publishing Company, 1984.

an explanation. The next thing we do is to look for it, without being too quick to accept any flippant explanation that comes along just so we can get out of a dilemma. If we were detectives, how would we begin to solve this mystery? The only thing that I can think of is to get a good Bible Atlas and see if we can find the Lake of Gennesaret.

The northern part of the Sea of Galilee was very near the city of Gennesaret. As a matter of fact these particular waters were often referred to as the "waters of Gennesaret". (They were also known as the waters of Chinnereth). When Luke referred to this part of the Sea of Galilee, he referred to it as the "Lake of Gennesaret". In other words, they are actually talking about the same place. We do the same thing today when we refer to areas with which we're familiar. If I were telling a story, I might say that it happened at Seven Lakes. My friend Terry Turner might say that it had occurred on the West Side. Although both of us would be correct, someone not familiar with this part of the country would believe we had contradicted each other.

What about the second **apparent** disparity? This one is actually a little simpler. Everyone who tells a story tells it a little bit different from the next person. Some put in lots of detail; others just skim over the details and present the highlights. That is exactly what has happened here. There is nothing here that makes it impossible for both of these passages to be true. Luke simply recorded (much) more detail than Matthew did. And you know what? Even that should strengthen our faith. Matthew was a tax collector. He took great pains to account for the claims of Christ. He carefully documented how Jesus' words fulfilled prophecy. He was more concerned with detailing these types of things than in describing every detail of routine events.

Luke on the other hand was a physician. He seemed to be more detail oriented in his writing about certain events. Remember that Luke tells us that his knowledge of the events he wrote about in the book of "Luke" were not from firsthand knowledge, but rather were from reports of persons who were eye witnesses[53].

> **NOTE**: Don't think for one minute that the fact that Luke was not an eye witness - in any way makes his writings invalid. The fact that he got his information from various sources does not invalidate divine inspiration. When the persons who penned the Bible wrote, they were guided by the Spirit of God[54]. That is where our claim of infallibility comes from.

Are there any other **apparent** inconsistencies in the Bible? Yes there are (a bunch), and we'll look at a few of them. Look at the following two passages – talking about the same thing, Jesus' instructions to his disciples:

Matthew 10: 9. Provide neither gold, nor silver, nor brass in your purses, 10. Nor scrip for your journey, neither two coats, neither shoes, nor yet staves: for the workman is worthy of his meat.

Mark 6: 8. And commanded them that they should take nothing for their journey, save a staff only; no scrip, no bread, no money in their purse: 9. But be shod with sandals; and not put on two coats.

Matthew says they should not take shoes, or staves (Staffs). **Mark** clearly says that Jesus commanded them to wear sandals and take a staff. How could this be? This is a good example of when we need to return to the original language. It is also a good example of something that we would be silly to fight over[55]. The reason that we want to clear this up, (besides

---

53   Luke 1: 1-2
54   2 Peter 1:21
55   1 Corinthians 1:10; 1 Corinthians 11:16

wanting to know all we can about scripture), is so that we can learn how to explain these types of <u>apparent</u> errors to non-believers.

*In **Matthew**, the Greek word for* shoes *is Strong's Ref. # 5266 Romanized hupodema Pronounced hoop-od'-ay-mah from GSN5265; something bound under the feet, i.e. a shoe or sandal: KJV--shoe.*

*In **Mark**, the Greek word for* sandals *is Strong's Ref. # 4547 Romanized sandalion Pronounced san-dal'-ee-on neuter of a derivative of sandalon (a "sandal"; of uncertain origin); a slipper or sole-pad: KJV--sandal.*

Let's discuss the difference between shoes and sandals. Sandals were regarded as a much less pretentious form of footwear. Obviously, Jesus wanted His followers to be, and to appear to be, as humble as possible – even down to what they wore on their feet.

How do we explain the difference in the instruction concerning the staff? I admit it took me a while to figure this one out – but there <u>is</u> an answer. Having a staff in one's possession was OK, since it was considered a walking tool. Having more than one staff was an indication that you were prepared to use one or more of them as a weapon. Jesus clearly did not want His followers to appear armed. Notice that **Matthew**'s wording prohibits plural (staves) while **Mark** permits the singular (a staff only). Also – if you do a search for "staves" you will find that in every case – a stave is considered a weapon.

Bottom Line

For hundreds of years the bad guys have been trying to discredit God's Word. King Jehoiakim took a knife, slashed

Scriptures to pieces, and tossed them into a fire[56]. In the Middle Ages those in power did everything they could to keep average persons from getting a copy of the Bible. Persons caught with scriptures were routinely tortured to death. The French philosopher Voltaire (1694-1778) made the statement that within 100 years of his death – all Bibles would disappear. Not only was he wrong – but – sadly he now realizes just how wrong he was.

---

56   Jeremiah 36: 22-23

Chapter Twelve

Listening to the <u>messenger</u>:

When we set in church and listen to what the Pastor says to us, we often make a *mistake*. The reason I put *mistake* in italics is that I am not so sure that it really is a mistake, as much as a semi-conscious cop-out. For example, when we hear the Pastor tell us that we need to give ten percent of our income to God, it's easy for us to ignore him. When the Pastor tells us we should come to church, it's uncomplicated to pay no attention to him; after all, what can he do to us? He's just a man.

I'd like to take this opportunity to make your life a little more miserable than it already is and remind you that the Pastor's words (when he is teaching scriptural doctrine) are not his own. They are from God. God has given us a wonderful book of instructions called the Bible. Every doctrinal word the Pastor speaks comes from the Word of God. If we choose to ignore them we are not ignoring the Pastor – we are ignoring God. Stop right now and think about that. **We are ignoring God.** So – from this point on don't ever allow yourself to hear the Word of God taught or preached, and think to yourself, "*That is nice, but I'll ignore it. After all, that is just a man speaking*".

Ignoring God is not something we should take lightly by

any means. Besides the fact that we **will** face Him someday, we are missing many tremendous blessings. Not only are we missing some of the more obvious blessings, we might well be cutting ourselves off from the fellowship we would otherwise have with Him. We should keep this in mind in all we do, including our prayer life. After all, if the only time God hears from us is when we need something, shouldn't that bother us just a little? I love my son dearly. If he grew up and left my house, ignored all advice I ever gave him, lived a life in complete contrast to what my wishes were and only contacted me when he had a need – what kind of a relationship would that be? I'd have to be pretty naïve to believe that he really loved me and craved my companionship.

Hearing everyone/thing <u>but</u> God: God has never spoken to me in an audible voice, but He has spoken to me. He has spoken to me many times, and I expect to hear from Him a lot more. Sadly, I imagine He has spoken to me lots of times when I chose not to hear Him. I didn't hear Him because I was too busy listening to everyone else. Take a second and be totally honest. When we are making an attempt to decide something in our lives, how much time do we spend (in prayer) talking to God about it? If it is really important we might spend ten minutes. We'll spend hours and hours talking to others. We'll talk to our spouse (and of course we should), our friends, Pastor, even folks we're standing in line with. I've heard strangers in the barber chair talk about a job change they are contemplating, and ask other strangers their advice. But we spend ten minutes, if that, talking to God.

Once we do spend our ten minutes talking to God, how much time do we spend <u>listening</u> to Him? How much time do we spend seriously trying to figure out what His will is? Do we go to Him in a quiet atmosphere, read our Bibles, and truly seek out His wishes?

Having the wrong motivation: This one seems obvious at first glance, especially since we have discussed it so much already. As if things weren't difficult enough, sometimes our motives are not so great as we think they are – even when we are doing the obvious work of God. Our ultimate example is Jesus. He is the one we should model our lives after. If we truly followed that tenet, imagine how different our lives, not to mention our church would be. This one calls for an example:

Let's pretend that God called a Pastor to start a church in a small community. Like most churches this one struggles at first and has it's share of ups and downs. As a matter of fact the church struggles a lot. Twenty-five years go by and the church never grows past one hundred members. The Pastor prays, and listens to God, and is convinced that he is doing what God wants him to do. What should that Pastor think about the lack of growth? Should he decide that he is obviously not doing what God wants because the church is not growing? Should he decide that he could do a lot more good if he were to take his talents and his abilities to a larger church, or at the very least move to a more populated area?

If God called that Pastor, we all know that the Pastor should stay right there. Here is the key. That Pastor does not even have the right to be discouraged. He's doing what God wants him to do. When he begins to be disappointed about church size, lack of growth, lack of funds and other human things – he is taking a bigger role upon himself than God intended. There is a reason that God wants that church in that area. None of us can possibly know the reason. There might be one person who will be reached that will eventually make a difference, but then again, there may not.

How does the above example apply to us? It applies in a couple of ways. If God has called us to a task, we have no right to question it using human standards. We have no right to get discouraged and quit if someone ridicules us, or if someone says something to make us angry. As a matter of fact – we don't even have a right to get discouraged. When we do - we are telling God that no matter what he has for us, we intend to use our standards, not His, to determine whether or not we are doing what we should.

Let's take this a step further. Sometimes our motives can even lead us to not (truly) obey God because we serve Him more than He is asking. (What?) Explanation: If a person works in the nursery, does AWANA, wonderful Wednesday, teaches Sunday School, visits, and does Children's Church, that person <u>might</u> be taking on too much. As if that isn't enough of a kick in the behind, they might be doing it with what they believe are good motives. Here is the ultimate question: "Am I doing what God wants me to do, or am I doing what I (as a human) have determined that is what God wants me to do?" Before we take a job in the church we should determine that is what God wants us to do. Is it so hard for our egos to believe that God may not want us to take every job that comes along?

> **Note:** I am a prime example of this. In the past I've gotten discouraged in AWANA, Children's church, and the Bible Time kick off. I was dead wrong. It makes no difference what I liked or didn't like about them. I was supposed to be serving the Lord strictly for the joy and the honor of serving Him. There are only two possibilities. **<u>One</u>:** I was doing what God wanted and it didn't make a bit of difference whether I liked it or not. **<u>Two</u>**: I was doing what <u>I</u> wanted, and I had no business there in the first place. My chief motivation for service should be my love for the Lord.

> **Note 2:** Please don't use this as an excuse <u>not </u>to serve God. Ask yourself, "Does He want me to serve?" I can answer that for you, "Yes – He does". Your task is to determine where He wants you and to follow that calling.

Final thought on this subject. If we are attempting to walk with God we can easily find ourselves attempting to "keep up" with Jesus. Common sense is a wonderful gift that God has given to all of us, and we should use it. A desire to serve is wonderful. So is a selfless commitment, and an eagerness to serve. The point is – we need to seek out **His** will, comply, and stay in touch with Him. We have no right to get discouraged as long as we are following these principles. When we do we are saying, "God – you have made a mistake. I don't know why I'm in this job, but it is obvious You did not know what You were doing. People are complaining, people are criticizing, no one is showing up, and I'm getting sick of it. To show You how little you know Lord, I'm seriously thinking of quitting this job that you mistakenly gave me. Remember - you are not your own – you are His[57].

Not trusting God during trying times: This is not a favorite topic of mine, because it is a tough one. It is hard to trust God when things are tough. It's easy when things are going fine. When things get really tough, it's gets right near to impossible to keep our faith all of the time. It is easy to doubt God, to look to man for remedies, to question our salvation, to wonder if we are being punished, and to have all kinds of other questions. Here is the key question in this chapter: "Do I trust God – or am I putting my faith in other people, and in my own ability to solve problems?"

I work with a Christian who is going through a pretty tough time in his life. The solution to all of his problems would be simple. He has prayed for months for God to help him. God could easily solve the problem. We are not talking about divine healing, parting waters or any other spectacular type of miracle. His problem has a simple fix. He knows that sooner or later all will be well, but right now he is struggling, and I mean struggling. He has used this situation to develop a wonderful testimony. His attitude is that God is in control and that God knows what He is doing. My friend has determined that although he cannot understand why the Lord has chosen

---

57   1 Corinthians 6:19

to drag this situation out, He has, and that is the end of it. He still trusts the Lord. He does not make any effort to pretend that he is happy about the situation. He does not even pretend to know why this is happening to him. He simply states that "God knows what He is doing and this thing will end when it ends." He has decided to trust God. As a result, nothing that has happened to him has shaken his faith.

This attitude violates all human accepted wisdom. Our attitude is "We have got to worry about what we are going to eat. We have to worry about our jobs. We have to worry about ...life." I've looked and I can't find that in God's Word. Everything the Bible teaches is about trusting God[58].

> **Note:** I probably should not have to add this note, but I'm going to - just in case. We are required to take care of our families. We can't just set out in the street and wait for manna. God has provided ways and means for us to obtain things that we need. As I've stated many times, the Bible was written for ordinary people with normal intelligence. There is nothing in it that indicates we should set on our behinds and expect God to look after us.

We grow stale: Unlike bread, <u>our</u> staleness has nothing to do with age. (Thank goodness) The Bible is clear that we should Guard our relationship with God[59].

If we are counting on human or monetary encouragement to keep us motivated, we are wrong and we will soon grow stale.

We do not love God: We can talk all we want to. We can proclaim our love for the Lord in Sunday School, Church and even at work. What do our inner thoughts proclaim? Do we love the Lord enough to really and truly seek Him? Are we loving to God or do we have a one way street in which we

58   Matthew 6:25
59   John 17:22

expect Him to be loving to us[60]? Do we love Him enough that we are willing to go anywhere He leads – no matter what the cost to us? Is our service based on this love or is it based on what we can get out of it[61]?

---

60   Jeremiah 2:2
61   Matthew 13:22

Chapter Thirteen

Is Fear a Sin?
(As if I didn't have enough to be fearful of)

Some people would answer the question by saying "Yes, it is definitely a sin. It shows a lack of faith and illustrates the fact that you do not trust God." Others would say "Of course it is not a sin. How could it be, we can't help it?" In this chapter we'll look at what the Bible says and see if we can come to a conclusion.

Philippians 4: 6. *Be careful for nothing; but in every thing by prayer and supplication with thanksgiving let your requests be made known unto God.* **7.** *And the peace of God, which passeth all understanding, shall keep your hearts and minds through Christ Jesus.*

8. *Finally, brethren, whatsoever things are true, whatsoever things are honest, whatsoever things are just, whatsoever things are pure, whatsoever things are lovely, whatsoever things are of good report; if there be any virtue, and if there be any praise, think on these things.* **9.** *Those things, which ye have both learned, and received, and heard, and seen in me, do: and the God of peace shall be with you.*

Verse 6 says to *"Be careful for nothing"*. This is another of those times when it is helpful to go to the Greek and find out what *careful* means. We find it is from the Greek word merimnao and means to be anxious about. (If you are interested it is Strong's reference #3309.

The scripture tells us to be "anxious about nothing". At first glance it sounds like it is saying that we are committing sin **any** time we become anxious. We have studied the Bible enough to know that this could not possibly be what it means. How do we know this? For one thing, we know from the example of Jesus. We know that Jesus was without sin. We also know that He was concerned about the trial He was going to face just before His crucifixion[62].

We can mince our words all we want and say that Jesus was not anxious. We can try to say that He was not concerned. The truth is that we can not avoid the fact that yes, Jesus was very concerned about the upcoming events. He handled it the way that we should – and we'll return to His example after we take a look at some other scriptures relating to worry.

John 14: 25. *These things have I spoken unto you, being yet present with you.* **26**. *But the Comforter, which is the Holy Ghost, whom the Father will send in my name, he shall teach you all things, and bring all things to your remembrance, whatsoever I have said unto you.* **27**. *Peace I leave with you, my peace I give unto you: not as the world giveth, give I unto you. Let not your heart be troubled, neither let it be afraid.*

God never intended for us to be equipped to handle things <u>apart</u> from Him. That is why He gave us the gift of the *"Comforter, which is the Holy Ghost"*. No doubt things will happen in our lives that will cause us to be concerned. I use the example of imagining yourself in an airplane that is in a steep, uncontrolled dive for earth. Are you supposed to sit <u>and calmly read</u> a magazine and sneer at the other passengers

62   Matthew 26; Mark 14; Luke 22

because they are worried? Of course not. Ideally you would, in your terror, pray to the Lord for help. You should ask Him to pull the plane out of the dangerous pattern it was in. You should ask Him to allow you to survive. Above all – you should pray for His will to be done – and you should mean it. (And that is the hard part.)

The Bible tells us that Jesus was in such agony that "*his sweat was as it were great drops of blood falling down to the ground*"[63]. That is some pretty serious agony. Even though He was concerned, Jesus still prayed "*Father, if thou be willing, remove this cup from me: nevertheless not my will, but thine, be done*"[64]. When Jesus prayed "*thine will be done*" He meant it. We should mean it too.

The Bible tells us that as Christians we will be known by our fruit[65] and that we should strive to bring forth the kind of fruit indicative of a Christian. Scripture also lists some of the characteristics of that fruit.

Galatians 5:22 *But the fruit of the Spirit is love, joy, peace, longsuffering, gentleness, goodness, faith,*

One of the listed fruit of the spirit is peace. God intends for Christians to be at peace. There is no doubt about it. He does not intend for us to worry. He does not want us to lie awake at night and agonize over our problems. The good news is that He has provided a means for us to accomplish this seemingly impossible charge.

Remember that **John 14:27** says *Peace I leave with you, my peace I give unto you: not as the world giveth, give I unto you. Let not your heart be troubled, neither let it be afraid.*

---

63   Luke 22:44

64   Luke 22:42

65   Matthew 7:16 - 17; Matthew 7:20; Matthew 12:33; Luke 3:8; Luke 6:43 – 44; John 15:16;

John (JD) Zumwalt

Also:

Romans 5: 1. *Therefore being justified by faith, we have peace with God through our Lord Jesus Christ:*

Romans 8: 6. *For to be carnally minded is death; but to be spiritually minded is life and peace.*

Romans 15: 13. *Now the God of hope fill you with all joy and peace in believing, that ye may abound in hope, through the power of the Holy Ghost.*

Galatians 5: 22. *But the fruit of the Spirit is love, joy, peace, longsuffering, gentleness, goodness, faith,*

Philippians 4:7 *And the peace of God, which passeth all understanding, shall keep your hearts and minds through Christ Jesus.*

Hebrews 13:6 *So that we may boldly say, The Lord is my helper, and I will not fear what man shall do unto me.*

1 Timothy 2: 1. *I exhort therefore, that, first of all, supplications, prayers, intercessions, and giving of thanks, be made for all men;* **2**. *For kings, and for all that are in authority; that we may lead a quiet and peaceable life in all godliness and honesty.* **3.** *For this is good and acceptable in the sight of God our Saviour;*

NOTE: One thing needs to be clarified, and this is a good place to do it. This is <u>not</u> a discussion about avoiding responsibility. It is not about putting our head in the sand and pretending that everything is OK and that we have no problems. We must recognize it when we have a problem and display concern. We have certain obligations that we must address. Some of our problems we have no control over, others we bring on ourselves. No matter what, our

---

obligation is to handle all of our problems in a manner consistent with scripture. When we find ourselves in bed, unable to sleep night after night because of our fears, there are certain actions that we can take.

1. **Go to God** – This does not mean that we utter some quick little prayer just so we can say that we've prayed about it. It means to faithfully and genuinely take your fear to the Lord. You do this by talking to God. You do this by realizing that you are indeed appearing before our Lord, through Jesus Christ, and you are speaking to Him – and He is listening to what you are saying. Once you are in a frame of mind so that you are absolutely aware of your status in God's presence – you talk to Him. You tell Him what you are worried about. You ask Him for help and for release from your fear.

2. **Accept God's will** – Most of the time we pray we say "your will be done" or words to that effect. Every single word we utter to God should be carefully weighed for sincerity. If we pray to God and say "your will be done" and we don't mean it, do you think He is fooled? If we are truly committed to the scriptural principle that God's will <u>always</u> takes precedence over anything we want, we might not pray those words in such an offhanded manner. Once we are genuinely committed to God's will, no matter what the consequences, our fears will not seem so important. (In other words – desire what God wants more than what you want.)

3. **Talk it over with a fellow Christian** – In a lot of cases this might be your spouse, in other cases it would not. It might be the Pastor, a Christian counselor, a Deacon, or a Christian friend. Be sure that whether you are getting counsel, or giving it, you are not outside the Word of God. Be sure to include scripture and prayer. If someone comes to you with

a fear, remember that even though it may not seem like much to someone else, that fear is very real to the person who is experiencing it.

When do we cross the line from legitimate concern - to sin? I think there are a number of indications that we have crossed that line. All of the indicators need not be present. We decide that what we want is more important than what God wants. We pray and pray and pray and get zero peace. We live our lives in fear, rather than in the peace and the joy that God expects. We are in a constant state of un-happiness and anxiety, always afraid of something. In other words, when we go through our lives without the peace and the joy that God so obviously intended for us to have, we are showing our lack of faith, and that is not what God wants. He wants us to live in peacefulness of heart.

Bottom Line

While we are on earth, we will always have fears. We will never have lives that are perfect and without problems. This is true no matter how wonderful our children may be, no matter how much money we have, and no matter how picture perfect our personal lives may be. We will have problems and we will have fears. We must face certain obstacles and figure out how we will overcome them. We will be on earth for just a short time. While we are here we must concern ourselves with living for the Lord as best we can, attempting to obey all scripture. That obedience includes trusting God to be there when we need Him, and trusting Him to overcome our fear.

Chapter Fourteen
Long Term Witnessing

How do we witness to people? How many times have we heard this topic discussed? In this chapter we are going to thrash out different aspects of witnessing – including some that we don't think about too often. I want to take a look at the people we attempt to minister to over a long period of time; the ones who we have been praying for and working on for years. This is a difficult chapter because it is going to cause us to take a tough look at some of the things that we do. Some of the things that we do with good intentions, might not be the <u>best</u> thing we could do at the time. Surprisingly enough we possibly will find that the right thing to do – is also the easiest. ***Question*** - What are some of the things we should know or some of the actions we should take? Please bear with me while I try to put this into some type of coherent order:

1. ***Know what it takes to get to heaven*** – It would be pretty sad if you found yourself in a situation in which you had the opportunity to lead someone to Christ and you did not know how. You might be thinking this is not worth mentioning because any Christian knows what it takes to get to heaven. No doubt,

every Christian (by definition) **does** know how to get to heaven. The question is, do we know how to <u>tell</u> someone else what they need to do? We'll cover this first. I've listed a **few** scriptures below that will help. I urge you to look at these and other scriptures and to practice when you are alone. Rehearse what you need to say so that when the opportunity presents itself you are ready.

Romans 3:23 *For all have sinned, and come short of the glory of God;*

Romans 5: 8 *But God commendeth his love toward us, in that, while we were yet sinners, Christ died for us.* **9** *Much more then, being now justified by his blood, we shall be saved from wrath through him.*

Romans 10:9 *That if thou shalt confess with thy mouth the Lord Jesus, and shalt believe in thine heart that God hath raised him from the dead, thou shalt be saved.*

Romans 10:13 *For whosoever shall call upon the name of the Lord shall be saved.*

2. ***Folks who do not attend church always have a reason that they don't*** – Let's get something straight right off the bat - <u>Everyone **needs** to go to church</u>. But obviously if you are trying to witness to someone who does not go to church, it is not going to do much good (in most cases) to quote scripture to them explaining that the Bible says we should. However, the following scriptures might be useful in witnessing to folks who tell you that they are Christians, but that they have decided to quit attending services.

Acts 20:28 *Take heed therefore unto yourselves, and to all the* *flock, over the which the Holy Ghost hath made you overseers, to feed the church of God, which he hath purchased with his own blood.*

1 Corinthians 11:22 *What? have ye not houses to eat and to drink in? or despise ye the church of God, and shame them that have not? What shall I say to you? shall I praise you in this? I praise you not.*

1 Corinthians 14:12 *Even so ye, forasmuch as ye are zealous of spiritual gifts, seek that ye may excel to the edifying of the church.*

Ephesians 5:25 *Husbands, love your wives, even as Christ also loved the church, and gave himself for it;*

Ephesians 5:29 *For no man ever yet hated his own flesh; but nourisheth and cherisheth it, even as the Lord the church*

Hebrews 2:12 *Saying, I will declare thy name unto my brethren, in the midst of the church will I sing praise unto thee.*

As previously stated, those who don't attend always have some reason why they do not. Some people will tell you that it cuts into their golf time. Others might tell you that they went when they were kids and it was so boring that they decided they'd never go back once they became adults and didn't have to. Some people frankly admit that they have no use for the Christian religion. There are hundreds of reasons that people can give, and be completely sincere, that explains why they do not attend church – ever.

Our challenge is to overcome this. In some cases all it will take is a simple invitation. Others will obviously be much more difficult. We don't want to badger them. All of us know that this tactic is ineffective and can do more harm than good. Another mistake we can make is to give people the feeling that they have a driving need, and we are smarter than they are because we know what it is. If someone gets the feeling that they are our little pity project they are gonna get fed up with us pretty quick. Remember that it is possible to truly be a friend to someone without having to witness to them <u>every second</u> of the time you are with them.

There are folks who will say, "That is wrong. If someone is lost, you need to talk to them about the Lord every time you see them." Go ahead and take that attitude. The problem is – you won't get that many chances to witness. They will soon be avoiding you like the plague. Then you'll be able to set in church and think to yourself what a wonderful Christian you are because the heathens steer clear of you.

Try to talk to the person. Try to get them to tell you what they have against church. Don't let Satan use anger to ruin your opportunity. (**2 Corinthians 2:11** *Lest Satan should get an advantage of us: for we are not ignorant of his devices.*) Really listen to the person. Tactfully answer their questions and respond to their doubts. You might find that they are perfectly willing to give church a shot. Statistics tell us that one person in four will attend church, if we just ask them. These same statistics indicate that the average number of invitations it takes is three. This brings up another point that we need to consider. Often we forget that, while we always want to encourage people to attend church, there are some services that are more appropriate for persons you are trying to lead to the Lord. **Example**: On the rare occasion when my Pastor preaches on stewardship, he always announces his subject well in advance. If you know that is the topic, why invite someone to church on that particular day? Especially if it is likely that is the only time they'll ever attend. Most of our services contain a Gospel message that outlines the need for salvation. That is the kind of message that would be valuable to a person you are attempting to witness to. If – the one time they attend church in ten years – they hear the Pastor appealing for money, they probably will have the attitude of, "That is exactly what I thought. All they care about is my cash." (**Mark 4:15** *And these are they by the way side, where the word is sown; but when they have heard, Satan cometh immediately, and taketh away the word that was sown in their hearts.*)

3. **Prioritize your message** – You may well be dealing with someone who has zero knowledge of the Christian message. It is possible that the person has some knowledge but believes it is just more hype. There are as many different ideas as there are people. If you are trying to talk to someone about their need for salvation, figure out where they are and treat them accordingly. (**1 Corinthians 3:2** *I have fed you with milk, and not with meat: for hitherto ye were not able to bear it, neither yet now are ye able.*) Someone who grew up in church, but who for one reason or another never accepted Jesus as their savior does not need the same message as a person who never went to a Christian church but is dabbling in other religions.

   We also need to take a look at the person's personal life. It would be ridiculous to walk up to a person who is a hard core drunk and tell them that all they have to do to straighten out their life is to say a prayer with you and then everything will be OK.

NOTE: As you know by now, it is my belief that the message that I call *Fairy Tale Christianity* can do lots of harm. A person who turns their life over to the Lord <u>can</u> deal with **anything** that comes their way. The fairy tale part is that it will happen by magic. The truth is that it will still be difficult. It will take prayer, study, faith, strength and courage. It will take time and it may involve setbacks. There is no magic prayer that guarantees that all of your troubles and all of your sadness and all of your addictions will suddenly disappear. The true message is of

---

a loving God who will guide us through this world with all of the tragedies that we might face. The real message is of an eternity in Heaven that is available to all of us by accepting the free gift He has offered to us.

4. **Live your life as an example –**

John 13:15 *For I have given you an example, that ye should do as I have done to you.*

1 Timothy 4:12 *Let no man despise thy youth; but be thou an example of the believers, in word, in conversation, in charity, in spirit, in faith, in purity.*

1 Peter 2:21 *For even hereunto were ye called: because Christ also suffered for us, leaving us an example, that ye should follow his steps*

This is something that is easy to understand and hard to do. If you are around someone all of the time they will get to know the <u>real</u> you. They will see you in the full range of your emotions. Satan has no better tool in his toolbox than the "bad example of a Christian". If a Christian is seen displaying uncontrolled anger, immoral talk or actions, or any other act that is not Christ-like, Satan will use it. He'll be right there on the person's shoulder whispering, "Oh yeah, they're great Christians. That's how they **really** act".

Acts 3:10 *And said, O full of all subtilty and all mischief, thou child of the devil, thou enemy of all righteousness, wilt thou not cease to pervert the right ways of the Lord?*

Here's the problem. We are humans. We try to be Christ-like and the longer we try the better we will do. The Bible is clear on this subject; we will not ever be sinless while we are on this earth.

Romans 3:23 *For all have sinned, and come short of the glory of God;*

Ħ When we err it is important that people around us understand that we try, but sometimes fail. My Pastor has said many times, if you do something to hurt your witness do not let any time at all go by. Do what it takes to correct it. If we react to something in anger, (**Ephesians 4:26** *Be ye angry, and sin not: let not the sun go down upon your wrath:*) do what it takes to make it right. If you hit your thumb with a hammer and scream out a curse word, (**Ephesians 4:29** *Let no corrupt communication proceed out of your mouth, but that which is good to the use of edifying, that it may minister grace unto the hearers*) explain that you were wrong and are working to get that particular sin out of your life. [Someone is going to say, "Oh, so you are saying that it is OK to cuss as long as you apologize?" NO – I am not saying that. Pay attention]

> **Note**: The best Christian man I ever knew was my Granddad. He read the Bible through <u>on his knees</u> 37 times. I don't ever remember seeing him in my life when he didn't have a Bible in his hand or by his chair. The IRS audited him because they did not believe he was giving most of his income to God's work. He spent most of the last years of his life witnessing to persons in jail or to street people. He started a Rescue Mission in his town and gave every spare dime and every waking moment to it. As good a man as he was, he was a sinner. He told me once that a neighbor who was revving his car engine up in the middle of the night had caused him to open the window and yell out a cuss word at the man. My Granddad, the best man I've ever known did that. He went next door and apologized and explained that he was human. He explained that he had come out of his sleep and acted inappropriately. He also explained that if the man did it again he would do something more

> appropriate (and Christian like). He told him he would
> file charges on him. As it turned out later – he did file
> charges. He knew that being a Christian does not mean
> you roll over and let people walk all over you – but it does
> mean that you act appropriately.

My granddad lived his life for God. Even now when I run into someone who knew him, the first thing they want to talk about is what a wonderful man he was. He knew how important it was that he do what was right <u>all the time</u>, so that none of the people who were watching him would not be hurt by his actions. When he cursed at the man next door he knew he was wrong. I think that what hurt him the most was his loss of witness. He taught me to always be aware of my actions, because "you never know who might not come to the Lord because of your actions". It is a difficult thing to do. Someday I hope to get it right.

1 Corinthians 8:9 *But take heed lest by any means this liberty of yours become a stumblingblock to them that are weak.*

1 Corinthians 8:13 *Wherefore, if meat make my brother to offend, I will eat no flesh while the world standeth, lest I make my brother to offend.*

Romans 14:13 *Let us not therefore judge one another any more: but judge this rather, that no man put a stumblingblock or an occasion to fall in his brother's way.*

5. <u>**Be a walking "Christianity Works" Billboard**</u> – This is very similar to being a good witness. When tough times strike you – lean on God. We often hear Policemen on the news saying that when a crisis occurred, instinct took over and they reverted to their training. That is exactly what we need to do as Christians. Remember that we're in school now.

We're learning things that will help us get through the tough times. All of the scriptural doctrines, all of the stories related by Christians we know, and all of the prayer that has been answered should be preparing us for the hard times that will come to us someday. Nothing speaks to a non-Christian like watching a Christian go through a crisis with God. We have a couple in our church who lost their son. When they suffered that horrible loss they handled it with such grace and with such trust in the Lord that a bunch of young folks were saved. Because of their faith – good came from something so terrible. (**Romans 8:28** *And we know that all things work together for good to them that love God, to them who are the called according to his purpose.*)

There is another part to this. We need to be there for folks who are suffering even if they are <u>not</u> part of our Church. Our Pastor's wife shared a testimony with us. She said that when she was a young girl her family was in danger of converting to Mormonism right after her mother died. She said that the Mormons were so good to them, and provided such a comfort that she feared for a while that her dad might convert. (Thankfully he did not) The point here is that Satan will fill any void we leave open, and he'll use it for his good. Our job is to deny him the opportunity. When our neighbors need Christian companionship and comfort – we should provide it.

Matthew 5:4 *Blessed are they that mourn: for they shall be comforted.*

John 14:18 *I will not leave you comfortless: I will come to you.*

2 Corinthians 1:3 *Blessed be God, even the Father of our Lord Jesus Christ, the Father of mercies, and the God of all comfort;* **4**

Who comforteth us in all our tribulation, that we may be able to comfort them which are in any trouble, by the comfort wherewith we ourselves are comforted of God.

6. **Do not be afraid of their questions** – There are folks who will have questions about Christianity. When they get to know you and trust you they'll open up and ask you about things that bother them. Do not be afraid to tell them that you do not know the answer to something. If you are unsure I suggest you do what I do – take time and look it up. If I still have a problem I'll turn to someone whose scriptural knowledge I trust, one of our Deacons or one of the Pastors or anyone else who I feel may be able to help me. The real point is do not assume that there is no answer. I don't care how tough a question someone asks, there is an answer. (I'm speaking here about someone who is sincere, not someone who is purposely playing games to prove that you are wrong.)

Colossians 4:6 *Let your speech be alway with grace, seasoned with salt, that ye may know how ye ought to answer every man.*

1 Peter 3:15 *But sanctify the Lord God in your hearts: and be ready always to give an answer to every man that asketh you a reason of the hope that is in you with meekness and fear:*

Be forewarned. Questions can range the full gambit from *"how could God have allowed my wife to die"*, to *"If there is a God, why does He allow innocent children to suffer"*? These are questions that have answers; in fact we've discussed them in our Sunday school class. Some things that non-believers might ask are hard to understand. I don't know why God did a lot of things, I just know that He did them. There are many things I don't understand, but it does not matter whether I do or whether I don't. This is where faith comes in. The problem comes when we use this as a cop-out. As Christians we know about God. We know what we have experienced. We know what He has done for us and for others. We feel His presence. The trouble is that a non-believer can't fall back on faith like we can, because they have no faith. Do not allow their arguments to hurt your faith.

1 Corinthians 2:5 *That your faith should not stand in the wisdom of men, but in the power of God.*

2 Corinthians 5:7 *(For we walk by faith, not by sight:)*

Ephesians 6:16 *Above all, taking the shield of faith, wherewith ye shall be able to quench all the fiery darts of the wicked.*

1 Thessalonians 3:7 *Therefore, brethren, we were comforted over you in all our affliction and distress by your faith:*

7. **<u>Try to get the person to read the Bible</u>** - They will not understand all of it. I know I **<u>still</u>** don't. Recommend parts of the Bible for them to read. The Gospels make wonderful reading and tell the story of Jesus. Talk to them about the actual suffering that Jesus went through. DO NOT forget to pray – always – for them that the Holy Spirit will work on them and that God will draw them to salvation.

John 6:44 *No man can come to me, except the Father which hath sent me draw him: and I will raise him up at the last day.*

Remember that Satan is going to do his very best to make sure they do not understand the scriptures you give them.

2 Corinthians 4:4 *In whom the god of this world hath blinded the minds of them which believe not, lest the light of the glorious gospel of Christ, who is the image of God, should shine unto them.*

8. <u>**Do not Compromise**</u> – It is tempting sometimes to yield a little to other people's beliefs. Do not allow that to happen to you. There are a lot of ideas being introduced by the New Age movement. Most of them are catching on because they are comforting. It is tough when someone looks at you and says, "*Are you telling me that my loved one will spend eternity in hell? They were good people and they believed that as long as you are a good person you would go to heaven.*" Responding to that is not easy. There are a couple of truthful responses that I'd like to submit. One answer is to say "*no one, not even my son or my daughter will go to heaven without accepting Christ*". That is the truth. As my Pastor often says, "God has no Grandchildren, only children." Another thing that gives me comfort sometimes is to hope that the person who has passed on accepted Christ as a child or at some other time without my knowledge. But always remember, Satan is good at holding out false hope – don't allow yourself to be sucked in to that trap in the interest of not hurting the person you are speaking with.

2 Timothy 3:13 *But evil men and seducers shall wax worse and worse, deceiving, and being deceived.*

1 Corinthians 3:11 *For other foundation can no man lay than that is laid, which is Jesus Christ.*

Ephesians 5:6 *Let no man deceive you with vain words: for because of these things cometh the wrath of God upon the children of disobedience.*

2 Thessalonians 2:3 *Let no man deceive you by any means: for that day shall not come, except there come a falling away first, and that man of sin be revealed, the son of perdition;*

9. **Never forget how important your mission is** – Time is running out. We have heard message after message from our Pastors about all of the signs that we are living in the last days. Even if the Lord tarries for two million more years, time is still running out. Every second that ticks is one less second that we will be on this earth. That last second – is the last chance to be saved. After death there is no such thing as praying someone into heaven, paying someone off, or pleading your case to God. The only chance anyone has is Jesus Christ – **now**.

Mark 1:15 *And saying, The time is fulfilled, and the kingdom of God is at hand: repent ye, and believe the gospel.*

Mark 13:32 *But of that day and that hour knoweth no man, no, not the angels which are in heaven, neither the Son, but the Father. **33** Take ye heed, watch and pray: for ye know not when the time is.*

10. **Don't hesitate to get help** – We have a whole churches full of fellow Christians who share your concern for your lost friend or lost loved one. We have prayed for several people in this church and we've seen the Lord save them. The question is, if we are called upon for help, what can we do?

❏ *Pray* – When we get these prayer requests they are not just something we do to be "church politically correct". This is real stuff and it is our duty to take it serious. When these requests are given out they come from folks who expect that we will go home and really pray, and that we will continue to pray.

1 Thessalonians 5:17 - *Pray without ceasing.*

James 5:16 - *Confess your faults one to another, and pray one for another, that ye may be healed. The effectual fervent prayer of a righteous man availeth much.*

Matthew 18:20 - *For where two or three are gathered together in my name, there am I in the midst of them.*

❑ ***Be prepared to visit if asked*** – Not everyone will be able to visit lost folks for the purpose of witnessing to them. Some folks would be comfortable making a visit and never mentioning the plan of salvation. That is perfectly OK. Your personality may not be suited (at least right now) for this type of ministry. You could make a visit to someone to let them know you enjoyed having them visit your church, or to let them know that if they haven't been there, you'd appreciate a visit from them.

There are folks in church who have a great talent for witnessing to people for the purpose of introducing them to the Lord. Some of you have the talent and don't even know it. Please consider getting out and getting involved with soul winning. This is a difficult thing for us to do. I'm not sure why it is so hard. In the United States about the worse thing that can happen to us is that someone will scoff at us or make fun of us. Satan has managed to make that sound horrible enough so that we avoid it.

Matthew 10-28 - *And fear not them which kill the body, but are not able to kill the soul: but rather fear him which is able to destroy both soul and body in hell.*

❐   **Greet each person who comes to your church** – The
church I attend has a reputation as a friendly church.
What I like about it is that folks here are friendly
because they are loving. We do not shake hands and
welcome people because of any ulterior motive, but
because we are sincerely glad they are visiting. Every
church should do the same. **Try to make it a habit to
seek out someone you believe is a visitor and shake
their hand and tell them you are glad to have them
as your guest**. I have visited churches where not one
single person said a word to me. Let me tell you, the
devil was right there pointing his bony little finger
at me saying, "These people don't want you here, I
wouldn't come back". If you don't believe it hurts a
church try going to a church and setting all alone –
with no one speaking to you.

1 Corinthians 16:20 *All the brethren greet you. Greet ye one
another with an holy kiss*

1 Peter 5:14 *Greet ye one another with a kiss of charity. Peace be
with you all that are in Christ Jesus. Amen.*

3 John 1:14 *But I trust I shall shortly see thee, and we shall speak
face to face. Peace be to thee. Our friends salute thee. Greet the
friends by name.*

> ***Note***: Paul told them to *"Greet ye one another with an
> holy kiss"*. In the interest of not being kissed by my good
> friends I'd like to say a few words about that passage. In
> Paul's time it was the custom for men to kiss men on the
> cheek. In the Middle East they still do this. [As a matter
> of fact when I tried to explain to them that in the United
> States (especially Texas) we don't do that, but that we
> hug the women, they could not believe it. They were

shocked that we would hug a female in public, especially not our wife, and <u>double especially</u> another man's wife. Meantime they are perfectly comfortable walking down the street holding another man's hand. (If you ever see me walking down the street holding David's hand please call an ambulance. One of us has had a stroke.) Paul is telling them to greet each other. In other words, shake hands – tell them you are glad to see them.

11. **<u>Do not be afraid to be honest</u>** – I have found that when you talk to folks about becoming a Christian or about attending church they are quick to bring up failures. They mention Jim and Tammy Baker, Jim Jones, or any one of the shyster evangelists who are out there today. When they bring them up I tell them, "There is no denying that we have had our share of losers. I admit it. This was predicted and we were warned to look out for these guys."

2 Peter 2:1 *But there were false prophets also among the people, even as there shall be false teachers among you, who privily shall bring in damnable heresies, even denying the Lord that bought them, and bring upon themselves swift destruction.*

The next thing to do is to point to the good guys in our Christian faith. There are a lot of them so it shouldn't be too hard. You can be sure that our own Pastors pass the test. My Pastor is a good example for folks who do not believe that it is possible for a Pastor to be earnest in their beliefs and their teachings as Clergymen. It is very important that we stand up and speak the truth about our Pastors. Do not let them be thrown in the same basket with the scum who have betrayed their calling. The work they do is imperative for carrying out God's work.

Romans 10:14 *How then shall they call on him in whom they have not believed? And how shall they believe in him of whom they have not heard? And how shall they hear without a preacher?*

BOTTOM LINE

I doubt if there is any Christian who does not have someone that they are concerned about for salvation. Most of us have friends or loved ones we've talked to for years that have rejected the plan of salvation. Some of these people are absolutely adamant about it. They will tell you that there is no way they could ever get involved in something like Christianity. I've heard a friend of mine say, "I will never believe that Jesus is the only way to heaven". The sad truth is that someday he will believe it.

No matter how difficult it may seem to you – do not give up on anyone. Do not give up. Winston Churchill made a famous speech once at a dinner. He got up, looked at the audience and said, "Never, never, never quit". Then he sat down. That is my advice about your lost friends or loved ones. NEVER QUIT – **you are their only hope. That is a tremendous responsibility.**

Matthew 18:11 *For the Son of man is come to save that which was lost.*

Matthew 24:13 *But he that shall endure unto the end, the same shall be saved.*

1 Corinthians 10:33 *Even as I please all men in all things, not seeking mine own profit, but the profit of many, that they may be saved.*

1 Timothy 2:3 *For this is good and acceptable in the sight of God our Saviour; 4 Who will have all men to be saved, and to come unto the knowledge of the truth.*

1 Timothy 4:15 *Meditate upon these things; give thyself wholly to them; that thy profiting may appear to all.* **16** *Take heed unto thyself, and unto the doctrine; continue in them: for in doing this thou shalt both save thyself, and them that hear thee.*

Chapter Fifteen

Thanksgiving

About 20 years ago I was doing some work that involved painting. I hate to paint, almost as much as I hate going to a drive thru window. I was painting the outside of a *Steak and Shake* in Houston, Texas. I had a little radio with me and I was listening to the local talk shows with earphones. I was not in the mood to talk to anyone; all I wanted to do was to get the job finished and leave.

While I was painting I noticed a man pull in to the parking lot riding a little Moped looking scooter. He was missing some teeth, his hair was all nappy looking, and he looked like he might have been sick. He also looked like he wanted to talk. I didn't want to talk to anyone – especially this guy. Fortunately for me God had other plans. I managed to avoid the guy on his way in, but on the way out he cornered me. I had to take the earphones out to speak to him. He started up a conversation and taught me a lesson I have remembered all of these years.

This fellow was a diabetic. His kidneys did not work which meant he could not use the bathroom. He had to go through dialysis a couple of times a week. He was weak, got out of breath easily, and could not perform much in the way of physical activity. He told me that he used to be a bread man.

He said that he had to get up early in the morning and load his bread truck, drive it all day, and deliver to various grocery stores. He told me how he used to gripe and complain and wish he could lay in bed and relax. He told me how much he hated that bread truck.

His life had changed. He said that things that meant so much to him several years before meant nothing to him now. He said, "You know, I would give anything I have if I could just get up for one day, load that bread truck up and deliver bread all day. One day, that's all I'd ask for." He told me that he remembered how good he used to feel. How great it would be to be able to lift those heavy loads and sling them onto the truck. Then he told me the one thing that has really stuck with me. He said, "People are thankful when things go their way. They are thankful for a new car or a good job. They forget to be thankful that they can move their arm, or breathe, or in my case – just go to the bathroom. You just don't know how much I would give to just be able to pee."

Now I realize that some folks might snicker or think that is too crude for a Christian book. If you'd seen him you wouldn't think that. That guy made an impression on me and I'll never forget him. He reinforced the lesson - that we are blessed and that we have so much to be thankful for. All of the problems that seem so major to us right now could become minor tomorrow. Tomorrow could bring tragedy to our lives, just like it did to the fellow in my story.

This chapter is a simple one. I just wanted to discuss the business of thankfulness. My goal is for all of us to come to the realization that we have got so much to be thankful for. I don't want this to be another trite cliché ridden bunch of words. I'm hoping that we will have an attitude adjustment that will carry us through our lives – in good and bad times. Besides the fact that we truly do have a lot to be thankful for, it is our duty as Christians.

1 Thessalonians 5 18 *In everything give thanks: for this is the will of God in Christ Jesus concerning you.*

I believe that the Bible means just exactly what it says. I don't believe that God used one word when He really meant something else. The verse clearly says, *"In everything give thanks"*. That does not require a lot of explanation. If we tried to write down everything we had to be thankful for, I don't think we could. Everywhere your eyes glance, there is something to be thankful for. There are people we know, places we've been, circumstances we've shared, and yes – even tragedies that God has allowed in our lives[66].

Jesus was our example. He gave thanks before eating[67]. We should do the same. When Jesus offered up a prayer of thanks, He did it sincerely. He did not do it so that the folks around Him would be impressed. On the other hand He was not embarrassed that they might laugh at Him. Obviously we should do it the same way. I said obviously, but we don't always do it that way. If we are with Christian friends we make sure that we pray, because we don't want them to talk bad about us. If we are with non-Christian friends we make sure <u>not</u> to pray because we don't want them to talk bad about us. One of my concerns about saying grace is that if we are not careful it can turn into a legalistic requirement. We find ourselves setting down to eat and yelling, "Wait a minute – don't eat yet, we haven't prayed." We yell that out like God is going to strike us dead if we eat and forget to pray first. Thankfulness is an attitude. You are not thankful just because you say "Thank you." I believe that being truly appreciative is a quality that Christians should have, and the more we realize how God works in our lives, the more thankful we should be.

All of us know that Thanksgiving and Christmas are some of the toughest times for those who do not have a whole lot. It

66   James 1:2-3
67   Matthew 15:35; Matthew 26:27; Mark 8:6; Mark 14:23; Luke 22:17; John 6:11

is also a tough time for those who must go through their first Christmas without a loved one that has passed on. When I tell you my heart goes out to those folks I sincerely mean it. I can't help but think about them. I also know that even they have an awful lot to be thankful for. I don't want you to read this and think, "What a tired statement. How can you tell miserable people that they have a lot to be thankful for?" The truth is, they do have a lot to be thankful for.

We have a lady who struggles into our church every week. When she finally makes it down the aisle to her seat and sits down, you can see her grimace for just a second because the pain is so bad. When she opens her mouth the only thing that comes out are words of thankfulness. And by the way, that mouth always has a smile on it. While we are on that subject, we recently lost a dear lady in our church family. No one ever heard her complain – ever. Her life changed completely, yet anytime you talked to her she had something good to say, and she always says it with a smile. The truth is – if you want to hear someone in our church whine and complain, you have to go find someone who has it pretty good.

BOTTOM LINE

We celebrate a Thanksgiving season. We celebrate the birth of Jesus. I'd like to see us take a minute or two, and decide that we will have a real attitude of thankfulness, not a pretend attitude. All of us have lots (yes LOTS) to be thankful for. If nothing else will make you realize that fact, just remember where you'll be in about 75 years or less. That ought to cheer you up. By the way, if it doesn't, I hope you'll give someone an opportunity to speak with you about it…

Chapter Sixteen
Lies – Is it Ever OK?

This is a subject I want to take a look at from a little different angle. This is an area that is under discussion among modern Christians, and is starting to be debated more and more. The question is, "Is there <u>ever</u> a time that a Christian <u>should</u> tell a lie?" Let me give you a set of circumstances to think about.

Imagine that you have a little girl who lives next door to you. You were there the day she was born, and have been good friends with her and her parents all of the girl's life. In our little story we'll say that the girl is really pretty, but does not have a whole lot of self confidence. On the night of the senior prom she knocks on your door. She has her date with her and she says to you, "I wanted so much for you to see me before I left. You know how much I love you, and how much it means to me to hear what you think. Do you like my hair, my make-up, and my dress? How do I look?"

You are in a dilemma because the truth is that she looks horrible. The dress is horrendous, the hair is awful, and the make-up looks like a clown. Now – one more addition to my story. This girl is no dummy. She knows your little trick about saying things like, "Honey, you are always beautiful to me."

She won't fall for "Your fingernails are lovely." She wants to know how you think she looks. What do you do?

You really have only two choices here. The first is to tell her the truth. "Sweetheart, you know I love you – but – you look awful. You need to contact a lawyer and sue whoever dressed you tonight." Then when she leaves in tears and you have ruined one of the most important nights of her life, you can think to yourself, "What a good Christian I am".

Your other choice is to lie and tell her that she looks gorgeous. She would not be hurt - but - doesn't the Bible mention something about lying?

Proverbs 14: 5 *A faithful witness will not lie: but a false witness will utter lies.*

Proverbs 12: 22 *Lying lips are abomination to the Lord: but they that deal truly are his delight.*

If we exercise choice number two and lie to that sweet girl, aren't we violating what God has written? We know that God does not / can not lie.

Titus 1:2 *In hope of eternal life, which God, that cannot lie, promised before the world began;*

So, what do we do!? This might be a good time to define lying. The last thing that we want to try to do is to get by on a technicality. That works fine with politicians and in court, but I don't want to be in a position of trying to get by with it when I face the Lord. However, we do need to know what we are talking about.

There are several definitions of "lie" but they all mean pretty much the same thing. Merriam-Webster's Collegiate Dictionary gives this definition: "To make an untrue statement with the intent to deceive." The question we must ask ourselves is, "Does our motive for telling a lie, ever make it OK?" Let's look at another example, this time it's one that I did not make up.

Joshua 2: 3 *And the king of Jericho sent unto Rahab, saying, Bring forth the men that are come to thee, which are entered into thine house: for they be come to search out all the country. **4** And the woman took the two men, and hid them, and said thus, There came men unto me, but I wist not whence they were:*

In case you are having trouble understanding that, it is the story of a prostitute who hid two men of God. In order to keep them hidden she had to lie to the persons who were looking for them. Just in case you are thinking that it was not against the rules at that time, let's look at some more scripture:

Leviticus 19: 11 *Ye shall not steal, neither deal falsely, neither lie one to another.*

There is no doubt that the law had been given, and the lying was prohibited. So, what happened to Rahab as a result of this lie she told. Again we'll turn to scripture to find out.

James 2: 24 *Ye see then how that by works a man is justified, and not by faith only.* **25** *Likewise also was not Rahab the harlot justified by works, when she had received the messengers, and had sent them out another way?*

What is James saying here? He clearly tells us that Rahab was justified by her faith and by her works. The works he is speaking of includes the fact that she misled the folks looking for the two men. Does that mean that not only was she <u>not</u> punished for telling a lie but that she was <u>blessed</u>? That's a tough one – let's keep looking at what the Bible says.

Exodus 1: 16. *And he said, When ye do the office of a midwife to the Hebrew women, and see them upon the stools; if it be a son, then ye shall kill him: but if it be a daughter, then she shall live.*

17. *But the midwives feared God, and did not as the king of Egypt commanded them, but saved the men children alive.* **18.** *And the king of Egypt called for the midwives, and said unto them, Why have ye done this thing, and have saved the men children alive?* **19.** *And the midwives said unto Pharaoh, Because the Hebrew women are not as the Egyptian women; for they are lively, and are delivered ere the midwives come in unto them.* **20.** *Therefore God dealt well with the midwives: and the people multiplied, and waxed very mighty.* **21.** *And it came to pass, because the midwives feared God, that he made them houses.* **22.** *And Pharaoh charged all his people, saying, Every son that is born ye shall cast into the river, and every daughter ye shall save alive.*

The Pharaoh ordered the midwives to kill all of the male children that they delivered. The midwives didn't do that. In other words, they refused to follow his orders. When the Pharaoh asked them about it, they lied and said that the Hebrew women had already delivered their babies by the time the midwives arrived. Make no mistake – they lied. What did God do to the midwives? The scripture tells us that "*God dealt well with the midwives*". Again, not only did He not punish them for lying – but – He rewarded them for not killing the Hebrew male babies.

Let's look at a few more examples that might apply to us:

1. A young child comes to your house and says to you, "I can't wait to see Santa Claus. My mom and dad told me he is real. Is he real?"
2. This is one that has happened to me. I investigated a traffic accident in which a teenage girl was killed. The doctor told us not to tell the mother who was critically injured, because it could cause further harm to her. The mother asked me if I knew her daughter's status. I lied and told her that I did not know.
3. What about war time? We make every effort to deceive (lie to) the enemy.

4. Police often use deception to capture criminals. We see this all of the time in sting operations. A good example is when a police officer poses as a child on line, in order to catch a pedophile.
5. **Every** year we give the Pastor a surprise birthday party. During the course of this event we do our best to deceive him. We do this by getting him somewhere under false pretense.

We've taken a look at some situations involving deception, both from scripture and from our own lives. All of the examples have been in order to accomplish the **greater good**. Now let's look at some examples of lies used for evil purposes. First an example from scripture:

Acts 5: 1. *But a certain man named Ananias, with Sapphira his wife, sold a possession,*

2. *And kept back part of the price, his wife also being privy to it, and brought a certain part, and laid it at the apostles' feet.* **3.** *But Peter said, Ananias, why hath Satan filled thine heart to lie to the Holy Ghost, and to keep back part of the price of the land?* **4.** *Whiles it remained, was it not thine own? and after it was sold, was it not in thine own power? why hast thou conceived this thing in thine heart? thou hast not lied unto men, but unto God.* **5.** *And Ananias hearing these words fell down, and gave up the ghost: and great fear came on all them that heard these things.* **6.** *And the young men arose, wound him up, and carried him out, and buried him.*

In this passage Ananias was killed for lying to the Holy Spirit. Later his wife tried the same little trick and was also killed. There are a couple of points here. One is so obvious that I almost hate to state it: Don't lie to God – ever. That is about the stupidest thing we could ever do. He will know we are lying. (Duh) The second thing is this…even though we saw two examples earlier of God not punishing liars, He sure punished this one. He punished him with immediate death. This lets us know that when God said not to lie, He meant it.

Proverbs 6: 6. *These six things doth the Lord hate: yea, seven are an abomination unto him:* **17.** *A proud look, a lying tongue, and hands that shed innocent blood,* **18.** *An heart that deviseth wicked imaginations, feet that be swift in running to mischief,* **19.** *A false witness that speaketh lies, and he that soweth discord among brethren.*

Revelation 21: 8 *But the fearful, and unbelieving, and abominable, and murderers, and whoremongers, and sorcerers, and idolaters, and all liars, shall have their part in the lake which burneth with fire and brimstone: which is the second death.*

One of the most successful bad guys of all time used lies as a tool. *"By means of shrewd lies, unremittingly repeated, it is possible to make people believe that heaven is hell -- and hell heaven. The greater the lie, the more readily it will be believed."* <u>**Adolph Hitler**</u> He also said: *"The great masses of the people will more easily fall victims to a big lie than to a small one."*

Just for fun I've added a few lies that we tell sometimes:

1. I can quit anytime I want to.
2. Oh thank you so much, this is exactly what I wanted.
3. It was owned by a little old lady who only drove it on Sundays.
4. I enjoyed the lesson John. (I think God allows this one – even though it is blatant.)
5. Things will improve if you vote for me.
6. I won't tell a soul.
7. He/she is in a meeting/the shower/garage, etc.
8. No honey, I think she's ugly.

Mark Twain gave a lot of advice about the dangers of being lied to. One thing he said was "The big print giveth and the small print taketh away." That is truer today than it was when he was alive.

Bottom Line:

I am a hater of legalism. Folks who walk this earth hurting feelings and not worrying about the welfare of others - in the name of Christianity - make me sick. There is no way that I am saying it is OK to lie. I would like to offer a definition of "lie" that I feel is more appropriate:

To utter falsehood with an intention to deceive; to say or do that which is intended to deceive another, when he has a right to know the truth, or when morality requires a just representation.

We have looked at a few examples in which morality required that the truth <u>not</u> be told. No rational person would hesitate to mislead someone in order to prevent the rape of their loved one. No loving person would destroy someone's sense of self by telling them something that would devastate them. How could we fault a police officer for lying to catch a child molester?

So – what is the answer to our original question? God has commanded that we not lie. He has also given us examples from scripture. Do not ever make the mistake of believing that it is up to us to make the decision when to obey and when not to obey God's word, based upon what we think or what we feel. On the other hand, He has given us compassion, wisdom, examples, and scriptural guidance. It is our duty to do everything that we can to be sure that we are in accordance with His wishes and that we are following Christian scriptural principles. As our dear friend Jeannette would quote:

Proverbs 3:6 *In all thy ways acknowledge him, and he shall direct thy paths.*

Chapter Seventeen

Fellowship with the Lord

I heard a speaker the other day say, "most people only know enough about God to be disappointed with him." That is so true. We become Christians, go to church, tithe, get involved in AWANA or participate in the music program. The question is, do we really *get it*?

A lot of us spend years as Christians without any idea about Spiritual growth. This is a little different from the issue of discipling new Christians. I have been around a number churches in my life. If I had to pick one area where they are <u>all</u> lacking – I would say that they do not teach Christians the things we need to know. Yes – we study the Bible, we learn all of the Bible stories, and that is very important. We need however, to know how to relate that to our lives. The Pastors at my church realize how important it is for us to use what we learn in church to <u>guide us in our everyday lives</u>. Most churches believe this – but - they don't do it. Here is Jeannette's favorite verse again:

Proverbs 3: 5 *Trust in the Lord with all thine heart; and lean not unto thine own understanding.* **6** *In all thy ways acknowledge him, and he shall direct thy paths.*

I believe with all my heart that these two verses are enormously important if a person ever hopes to understand the relationship that it is possible for us to have with God - while we are still on this earth. Let's look at what the scriptures say we should do:

1. <u>*Trust in the Lord with all our heart*</u>. That means complete and total trust. It means that we have faith in God – no matter what. It means that we never say, "Sorry Lord, I'm jumping off because it just doesn't seem like you know what you are doing. I'm gonna make the decisions from now on." That brings us to:

2. <u>*Do not trust your own understanding*</u>. There are going to be times when we do not understand what we are going through. There will be times when we will feel like we need to take the reins and make decisions contrary to where we <u>were</u> trusting God to take us. This is where our faith **must** kick in. I can guarantee you that there is not a child in our church who has not had times when they didn't wonder, "What in the world are my parents thinking of? How can they possibly be so stupid as to ground me at such an important time as this?" That is exactly the same lack of trust we show God when we refuse to trust His decisions in our lives. We are saying the same thing that our children say to us, "I know more than you do about what is best for me".

   Now having said that, let me make another point. We live in the real world, not fantasy land. The truth is that it is awfully hard to not second guess God sometimes. It is difficult for us, with our pathetic lack of understanding, to deal with things occasionally. That's where faith comes in. That faith is what we should be developing <u>now</u>.

3. <u>In all of our ways we should acknowledge Him</u>. This

is easy to do while we are sitting in church. It can be incredibly difficult when we are at home, work or the grocery store. Notice that it says in **ALL** ways acknowledge Him.

4. Remember that God will direct our paths. This is the good part. God will direct our paths – if - we let Him. The scripture says, *"he shall direct thy paths"*. It does not say, *"close your eyes like an idiot and plunge blindly ahead"*. **We have some responsibility here**. This is the part I want to discuss in this chapter.

Note: This lesson is for all kinds of folks. There are some people who will not allow themselves to be happy, no matter what. They always, always have a crisis in their lives. Nothing you do, nothing you say can make them happy. I'm not speaking of those who have a clinical or medically diagnosed depression. I'm referring to Christians who have the attitude of "Woe is me. No matter what I do my conditions do not improve".   We also have the kind of person who is striving for happiness through the accumulation of things, or friends, or accomplishments, etc. They have not noticed yet that no matter what they get, no matter what they accumulate, they are not ever as happy as they'd like to be.

The lesson here is that the happiness that God has promised us has <u>nothing</u> to do with what we normally associate with cheerfulness. We cannot bribe God with our works to get a new car, a new house, or a new anything. The good news is that we can obtain a happiness that is unimaginable without God's presence.

It is my firm belief that <u>most</u> of us truly do want to do the (scripturally) right thing. Sometimes we just don't know what the right thing is. The reason that we don't is that we don't know enough about the Bible. Every single Christian is completely capable of taking the next step in their Christian walk; and then the next step, and the next, and so on. The problem is that not everyone will, no matter what the Pastor or other church members do. I promise you that as a Christian, the deeper you immerse yourself in the Word of God, and the closer your relationship with Him becomes, the happier you will be. Not because I say so – but because the Word of God says so.

Psalm 144: 15 *Happy is that people, that is in such a case: yea, happy is that people, whose God is the Lord.*

Psalm 146: 5 *Happy is he that hath the God of Jacob for his help, whose hope is in the Lord his God*

Remember, this chapter is directed at folks who have a relationship with the Lord. These verses and this advice will not do an unsaved person any good – (unless they get saved.) Sometimes we read these verses and we think, "Then why am I not happy? I go to church. I pray. I tithe, teach Sunday school, etc. Why am I so miserable?" These verses are telling us that we should have our <u>complete</u> trust in God. The first verse looks redundant doesn't it? What does it mean when it says "whose God is the Lord"? It means we can <u>believe</u> in God all we want. We can have 100% belief that He is alive and has the ability to save us and to guide us. As we've discussed in a previous chapter, the Bible tells us that for us to believe this is no big deal.

James 2:19 *Thou believest that there is one God; thou doest well: the devils also believe, and tremble.*

I guarantee you that Satan and all his demons have a faith that there is a God and their faith is unshakable. They **know** He is God. Their problem is that <u>He is not their Lord</u>. God must be our Lord. Just believing in Him will never take us to the next level that He wants for us. <u>Just</u> believing will never allow us the happiness that is available through Him. There is a joy in a relationship with God that can not be obtained any other way.

Psalms 51:12 *Restore unto me the joy of thy salvation; and uphold me with thy free spirit.*

These words were written by David. There is no way we can realistically hope to acquire more than David had. He had wealth and power beyond our wildest imagination. Because of his position he could have anything he wanted – ANYTHING. David discovered that all he possessed was worth zero, compared to the joy he got through his relationship with God. As a matter of fact, next time you feel burdened by sin, read the 51st Psalm. If you are not sure how to ask for forgiveness – this passage will teach you how. As David knew very well, with God's love and forgiveness comes the "joy of salvation". He also knew the converse – without God in our lives – we will be miserable.

I know there are some who would answer this by saying, "I'm not even a Christian and I am very happy". There are others who would say, "I'm a Christian and I'm not living the kind of life that I know I should, and I'm very happy". I would answer them by saying this. Some folks <u>think</u> they know what it means to be sad. They think that they have experienced grief because they have had a traumatic event in their life. Obviously there are those (even in our class) who have experienced horrific losses. They truly understand sadness. Unfortunately, there are others who will someday find out the **<u>true</u>** meaning of grief. They will understand the exact meaning of anguish, and when they do - they will understand that the sadness they experienced before was nothing.

Similarly, unless a person has experienced the true joy that can be realized through a real relationship with the Lord, that person can not understand the pleasure and happiness that can be had. God does not guarantee us that nothing bad will ever happen to us. He does guarantee that He will be with us when bad times strike. A loving father will hold his son or daughter during their time of grief. A loving wife will comfort a grieving husband. God will be there to comfort us – <u>if</u> we let Him.

Let's look at the next two passages of scripture, keeping the Bema Judgment in mind:

1 Peter 4:14 *If ye be reproached for the name of Christ, happy are ye; for the spirit of glory and of God resteth upon you: on their part he is evil spoken of, but on your part he is glorified.*

Matthew 10:28 *And fear not them which kill the body, but are not able to kill the soul: but rather fear him which is able to destroy both soul and body in hell.*

NOTE: At the Bema seat, all <u>Christians</u> will be judged (for rewards) at the same time. That means that we will be standing beside all types of Christians. Some got there by the skin of their teeth. There will be others who we will not feel worthy to even speak to. There will be thousands of martyrs present. That is the moment when we will truly understand what these passages mean. Those martyrs will face Jesus and He will know that they suffered and died for Him. Many of them died horrible deaths of unspeakable agony. They died that way because they loved Christ. All we have to endure in America is a sneer or a rude remark – and most of the time we're not even willing to do that. That is the "Martyrdom" that we'll take to the Bema. One important point: If we are faithful to endure the sneers for God, it is worth just as much as the death of those martyrs. Why? Because we are being judged for the circumstances **we are in**, and how well we do with what God **has given us.**

I've talked about the subject of Christian growth a lot in

this book. I want to re-visit some of these discussions and then go a step further.

1 Corinthians 3:2 *I have fed you with milk, and not with meat: for hitherto ye were not able to bear it, neither yet now are ye able.*

1 Peter 2:2 *As newborn babes, desire the sincere milk of the word, that ye may grow thereby:*

This is where it gets a little bit uncomfortable. When we are born again, the analogy of a baby and a new Christian fits. A baby needs milk. A baby does not always realize what he or she needs. Consequently, the infant is dependent on others to help. Similarly, a baby Christian needs the milk of the Word of God. This milk is required for growth. We start with this milk – because – like the baby, we can't handle solid food yet. Here is the uncomfortable part. There comes a time when we have to add meat to our diet if we ever hope to grow as Christians. (We don't stop drinking milk, but we do supplement it.) Do not allow yourself to become an old Christian and still be on a milk diet[68].

Hebrews 5: 12 *For when for the time ye ought to be teachers, ye have need that one teach you again which be the first principles of the oracles of God; and are become such as have need of milk, and not of strong meat.* **13** *For every one that useth milk is unskilful in the word of righteousness: for he is a babe.* **14** *But strong meat belongeth to them that are of full age, even those who by reason of use have their senses exercised to discern both good and evil.*

It is not enough to lie around and eat. We have to do some type of exercise if we are going to grow. A person who is bed ridden will start to lose muscle very quickly. No matter how much or how well they eat, if they do not exercise they will

---

68   Also see Matthew 4:4

not grow stronger. The Bible tells us that we need to exercise as well. We grow by eating <u>and</u> by exercising. It takes both. Just getting older does not mean that we will be more mature Christians.

1 Timothy 4: 6 *If thou put the brethren in remembrance of these things, thou shalt be a good minister of Jesus Christ, nourished up in the words of faith and of good doctrine, whereunto thou hast attained. 7 But refuse profane and old wives' fables, and exercise thyself rather unto godliness. 8 For bodily exercise profiteth little: but godliness is profitable unto all things, having promise of the life that now is, and of that which is to come.*

So what is the meat that we are speaking of here? What can we do for the Lord other than read our Bibles and learn all that we can?

John 4: 34 *Jesus saith unto them, My meat is to do the will of him that sent me, and to finish his work. 35 Say not ye, There are yet four months, and then cometh harvest? behold, I say unto you, Lift up your eyes, and look on the fields; for they are white already to harvest. 36 And he that reapeth receiveth wages, and gathereth fruit unto life eternal: that both he that soweth and he that reapeth may rejoice together. 37 And herein is that saying true, One soweth, and another reapeth. 38 I sent you to reap that whereon ye bestowed no labour: other men laboured, and ye are entered into their labours.*

Every Christian has a role in the harvest of souls. God expects this. It is our duty, it is our obligation. It is also part of the meat that helps us to grow as Christians. Do not misunderstand. Not everyone has the gift of soul winning. Obviously some folks are great soul winners. These are the ones who God has gifted with the ability and the circumstances to be able to lead folks to Christ, and it seems almost effortless. On the other hand, we all have an obligation in this area, and we have to be careful not to ignore it or to trivialize it. What can we do in the area of soul winning? Let's talk about just a few:

1. <u>We can pray</u>[69] –Two comments on the subject of praying for the lost. One is be to specific. Pray for individuals by name. Keep them on your list and don't let up on them. Pray hard and pray with faith. Never quit. Secondly, don't let the fact that you are praying be an excuse to do nothing else. Don't get the attitude of, "I'm praying for people, that fulfills my obligations toward the winning of souls".

2. <u>Invite people to church</u> [70]– When is the last time that you invited someone to church? Did you follow up with them? Did you really extend an invitation or did you just off handedly mention it to them? Please don't forget this important area of ministry. My prayer is that all of us will be burdened with the importance of asking people to join us at our churchs.

3. <u>Work to make church an enjoyable experience for children</u>[71] – Consider getting involved in AWANA or in Children's Church. At the Bema, some of you are going to find out that you had a tremendous impact on the lives of numerous people through the influence you had with children. When I see adults sitting quietly and listening to kids quote scripture, I always wonder if that adult has any idea of the impact they are making on that child. This is not particularly scriptural, but I can imagine a lot of these kids (and their parents) coming up to you in heaven and saying, "Thank you so much. You have no idea what a huge

---

69   Matthew 9:38
70   1 Corinthians 7:17; 1 Corinthians 10:32; 1 Corinthians 11:22; Revelation (Chapters 1-3)
71   Matthew 10:42; Matthew 18:6; Matthew 18:10; Matthew 18:14; Mark 9:42; Mark 10:13-14

influence you had on my life". I wish more folks would consider getting involved with children at your church as well; I guarantee you - they need the help.

4. <u>Work on making our witness as positive as is possible</u> – Every one of us understands the importance of being a positive Christian influence.

5. <u>Get involved with different ministries</u> [72]– There are many ministries we can get involved with. If you are looking for one, contact someone in your church leadership. Just in case you don't think you are able to do anything take a look at two folks I used to attend church with, Jean and Jeanette. Jeanette struggled sometimes to get around. She will be the first to tell you that she is not as agile as she used to be. Yet, she and Jean had a prison ministry they are faithful to. They went to the jail every Sunday night and witness to the prisoners. I'd say that is one of the toughest ministries in any church. If they can do that, we should have the confidence to go forward with <u>wherever</u> God leads.

6. <u>Work to make church an enjoyable experience for adults</u> – Greet visitors, shake hands and tell folks you are glad to see them. Do it like you mean it, but only if you do mean it. Do it not as a con, but as an act of love.

   Another obligation we have in our Christian growth is to glorify God[73]. All of our actions, <u>if we allow them</u>, can glorify God. I don't think there is anything that will destroy a good Christian ministry quicker than failure to give God the credit for it. So many men of God have turned into counterfeits because they began to enjoy the glory that THEY were getting – instead of giving it to God where it belonged.

---

72   Matthew 28:19&20
73   Matthew 6:2; John 7:18; Acts 12:23; Romans 4:20; 1 Corinthians 3:21; 1 Thessalonians 2:6;

1 Corinthians 3:18 *Let no man deceive himself. If any man among you seemeth to be wise in this world, let him become a fool, that he may be wise.* **19** *For the wisdom of this world is foolishness with God. For it is written, He taketh the wise in their own craftiness.* **20** *And again, The Lord knoweth the thoughts of the wise, that they are vain.* **21** *Therefore let no man glory in men. For all things are yours;* **22** *Whether Paul, or Apollos, or Cephas, or the world, or life, or death, or things present, or things to come; all are yours;* **23** *And ye are Christ's; and Christ is God's.*

Chapter Eighteen

Once Saved – Always Saved?

Baptist doctrine states that …"***All true believers endure to the end. Those whom God has accepted in Christ, and sanctified by His Spirit will never fall away from the state of grace, but shall persevere to the end.***[74]" This is the position of our Pastors and of course, our church. It can be a confusing topic, and is a good example of how verses can be difficult to understand - sometimes. The Bible tells us that we should be ready to explain our beliefs[75]. With that in mind we are going to look at the question of "Can a person who has been saved – lose their salvation?" Before we begin the discussion of whether or not salvation can be lost, let's agree on a few things:

1. There is only one way to salvation – <u>Jesus Christ</u>[76].
2. <u>Anyone</u> can be saved[77].
3. God must call us to salvation[78].

---

74   Article V – Basic beliefs – Official Web Page Southern Baptist
      Convention (http://www.sbc.net/aboutus/basicbeliefs.asp)
75   1 Peter 3:15
76   John 14:6; Romans 10:9;
77   Romans 10:13
78   John 6:44; Matthew 11:27; Luke 10:22; John 6:37

4. Everyone one of us is a sinner[79].
5. We are saved by faith – <u>not by works</u>[80].
6. We must realize that Jesus paid the price for our sins by dieing on the cross. He was offered as the final extreme sacrifice to pay for our sins[81]. <u>That fact must be accepted</u>. We must repent[82] of our sins, and ask forgiveness[83]. At that point – we have obtained salvation. There are arguments that a person must do other things as well, for example – be baptized. We believe that baptism is God's will; we do not believe that it is a <u>requirement</u> for salvation. That subject will have to wait for another chapter.

For the purposes of our discussion allow me to create a fictional character and call him Fred. Fred got up one day and realized that his world was falling apart. His wife notified him that she'd be a lot better off without him - and she decided she'd take the kids. (She left the dog.) When he got to work he found that he had been fired, because his wife had run off with the boss. You get the idea. Fred started to drink. Things got worse and worse and finally, out of extreme desperation, he decided he would visit a church. As soon as Fred walked in he began to feel a little better. Folks were kind. They greeted him at the door and he knew he was welcome. No one made any judgments about his personal or his financial status. Fred became emotional almost from the beginning

79   Romans 3:10
80   Ephesians 2:8-9
81   John 3:16; Romans 5:8; Romans 6: 7-11; Romans 14:10; 1 Corinthians 15:3; 2 Corinthians 5:14-16; 1 Thessalonians 5:9-10; Ephesians 2:16;
82   Matthew 3:2; Matthew 4:17; Matthew 9:13; Mark 1:4; Mark 1:15; Mark 6:12; Acts 3:19
83   Matthew 6:7-13; Acts 8:22; Acts 13:38; Acts 26:18; Romans 4:7; Ephesians 1:7; Colossians 1:14

of the service. He had to fight back tears during the congregational singing. When the special music was being sung he could hardly control his emotions. By the time the Pastor was finished speaking Fred was ready. During the invitation he quickly made his way forward and told the Pastor that he wanted to accept Christ as his savior. The Pastor questioned him and felt certain that Fred understood what he was doing.

A month or so later Fred was baptized. He came to church fairly regularly and attended Sunday school as well. Things began to improve for Fred. He met a lady, married her and went to work in a business that she owned. The better things got in Fred's life, the less they saw him at church. One day the Pastor had to accept the fact that Fred was not going to come back to the church. What he didn't know was that Fred was living a life that was far from what is expected of a Christian. He was getting drunk. He was running around on his wife. He was stealing money from the company. In short, Fred was living a life immersed in sin. Here is our question: **If Fred died right now – would he go to heaven or would he go to hell?**

The first and most obvious question is "Was Fred really saved? He said and did all of the right things. He had to be a Christian – right?" As always, let's see what the Bible says.

NOTE: Before we go any further I want to make sure that no one thinks that we are getting into the area of judging whether or not a person is saved. Sometimes we cannot help but have our ideas, but there is no way we can be certain about the salvation of others. There are indications of salvation and we will discuss those in this lesson. **God is the final and only Judge of the truth of salvation84.**

---

84   Matthew 7:1-2; Luke 6:37; John 8:50

We are going to ask the question "Is it <u>possible</u> that fictional Fred might not have truly been saved?" The answer is clearly – yes, it is possible. Unfortunately Satan is not an idiot. He uses a variety of tools and he has had a long time to learn how to use them. He can even use our emotions on us. I can not help but wonder how many people have been caught up in emotion during a meeting and run forward to make a profession of faith, only to forget their commitment a few days later. Christianity is not like signing a letter and joining the AARP. It is a commitment very much like marriage is a commitment[85]. There will be a change in the person who is saved[86]. The change will be obvious to them and in some cases – to others[87]. What is the lesson here? If you have accepted Christ as your Savior and there has been no change at all in your life, <u>you</u> should take another look at <u>your</u> experience.

> **Note:** One of the dangers in a discussion like this one is that Christians will start to doubt their own salvation. I encourage everyone who is saved to take a **one time** look at their salvation. The best time to do this is at the time you are saved. If you have not done it – do it now. Ask yourself this question: "Did I truly accept Jesus as my Savior and did I understand what that meant?" Once you resolve that question **<u>don't ever allow Satan to bother you with it again.</u>**

One possibility is that Fred did not have a <u>true</u> experience. He might well have thought he could *sign on the dotted line* and be assured of a place in Heaven. What a great victory for the devil if he can convince someone of that. I can't help but wonder if Fred knew what he was getting into when he professed Christ. Did he realize the commitment? We've used

---

85   Matthew 25:1; Mark 2:18-20; John 3:27-31; Revelation 18:23; Revelation 21:2; Revelation 21:9
86   2 Corinthians 5:17;
87   Matthew 3:8;Matthew 3:10; Matthew 7:16-20;

this example before, but it fits here. Can you imagine marrying someone and in a week or two having them announce to you that they had no intention of being loyal? That is exactly what happens when we "marry" Christ and then forget Him unless we need our "laundry done".

There are also folks who never were sincere in the first place. This is also scriptural[88]. This category includes anyone who enters into a ministry for financial reward or any other personal reason. It is my belief that many of the television evangelists fit in this group. This is a good place to point out that it is contrary to the Word of God to believe that you can obtain His gifts by sending money[89].

Another explanation for lack of salvation is illustrated in the story of the (as Pastor Ken calls it) prodigal pig.

2 Peter 2:22 *But it is happened unto them according to the true proverb, the dog is turned to his own vomit again; and the sow that was washed to her wallowing in the mire.*

I do not know a whole lot about pigs. I know enough about them to understand what this passage of scripture is saying. You can clean a pig up. You could invite it into your house, give it clean sheets to sleep in, and make sure it had the proper place setting at the dinner table. The pig would not be a bit impressed. The pig would much rather be out in the hog trough slopping around, and the first chance it gets it will return there.
The same is true of a person who never really understood the significance of becoming a Christian. A person who does not have an understanding of the value of the gift God has given us will be much more comfortable out in the world, doing the things that Satan provides for them. Just as surely as a hog will return to the environment it feels comfortable with – a

---

88   Matthew 24:11; Matthew 24:24; Mark 13:22; 2 Corinthians 11:13-15; 2 Corinthians 11:26; Galatians 2:4; 2 Peter 2:2; 1 John 4:1
89   Acts 8:20

person who has not made a true commitment will return to the lifestyle they are most comfortable with – count on it.

The question of backsliding can not be avoided here. Is it possible that a person can be saved and get out of the will of God? It is absolutely possible. It has happened to great men of God all through the Bible. God did not allow Moses to enter the Promised Land because Moses disobeyed Him[90]. When we read the story of David we have an example of a man who God loved dearly. David committed horrible sins, always returning with anguish and asking forgiveness. It is possible to do this but I'd be very leery to use this as an excuse. Don't allow someone to tell you that they are saved and living in sin - without asking them if they are <u>sure</u>. There will be some conviction by the Holy Spirit if they are indeed saved, and if they live long enough they will return, just as the Prodigal Son returned[91]. Persons who are saved and who are living in sin are, for all practical purposes, dead to the Lord. They have no communication with Him and certainly have no joy of His salvation. The only way to remedy this is to return to His will. It's time to address the issue of eternal salvation. Could Fred have been saved and <u>then</u> lost it? Let's look at scripture.

Romans 11:29 *For the gifts and calling of God are without repentance.*

The literal Greek is: |0278| <u>*without a change of heart*</u> |1063| *For* |3588| *the* |5486| *free gifts* |2532| *and* |3588| *the* |2921| *calling* |3588| *of* |2316| *God.*

In English or in Greek it is the same. It does <u>not</u> say "God gives us the gift of salvation but if you are not careful he will take it back." It clearly states that <u>all</u> of God gifts are given without *change of heart.*

Ephesians 1:13 *In whom ye also trusted, after that ye heard the*

---

90   Deuteronomy 34:4;
91   Luke 15:11-32

word of truth, the gospel of your salvation: in whom also after that ye believed, ye were sealed with that holy Spirit of promise, **14** *Which is the earnest of our inheritance until the redemption of the purchased possession, unto the praise of his glory.*

What I would like to do now is to take a look at some of the scriptures that <u>seem</u> to indicate that we <u>can</u> lose our salvation:

Galatians 5:4 *Christ is become of no effect unto you, whosoever of you are justified by the law; ye are fallen from grace.* In this verse Paul is writing to the church at Galatia and admonishing them for turning away from the doctrine of salvation by grace. He is not saying to them that they have lost their salvation – but rather that they have turned from the doctrine of "salvation by grace". The Galatians had been turning towards a doctrine of salvation by <u>works</u> and this concerned Paul.

Colossians 1:21 *And you, that were sometime alienated and enemies in your mind by wicked works, yet now hath he reconciled* **22** *In the body of his flesh through death, to present you holy and unblameable and unreproveable in his sight:* **23** *If ye continue in the faith grounded and settled, and be not moved away from the hope of the gospel, which ye have heard, and which was preached to every creature which is under heaven; whereof I Paul am made a minister;*

The argument has been made that in verse 23 Paul is saying that "<u>if</u>" a person continues in the Christian walk they will continue to be saved. This seems to imply that if they don't, they will lose their salvation. When you study Paul's writings you will notice that he uses the word "if" as we would use the word "since". It is not a condition but rather a method of argument and logic. Understanding this makes it clear that Paul is not indicating a threat of lost salvation.

James 5:19 *Brethren, if any of you do err from the truth, and one convert him*; **20** *Let him know, that he which converteth the sinner from the error of his way shall save a soul from death, and shall hide a multitude of sins.*

There is no indication here, either in English or in Greek that James is speaking of a person who was once saved and then lost their salvation. He is speaking of a person who rejected the truth and was convinced of his error. The person in this passage was converted, not re-converted. While we are on the subject of the writing of James let's take a look at another passage that seems to indicate that works are required for salvation.

James 2:14 *What doth it profit, my brethren, though a man say he hath faith, and have not works? can faith save him?*

At first glance this scripture seems to be saying that faith can not save us and that works is (also) required. This would be in direct contradiction to other passages in the Bible[92]. We know the Bible does not contradict so let's see if we can figure out what James is saying. We can do this by looking at the full passage[93]. We see that James is telling us that if someone needs help we may have to perform an **action**. Simply telling the person that we have faith does them no good, we have to show them. The passage is not dealing with the issue of salvation.

1 Corinthians 6: 9 *Know ye not that the unrighteous shall not inherit the kingdom of God? Be not deceived: neither fornicators, nor idolaters, nor adulterers, nor effeminate, nor abusers of themselves with mankind,* **10** *Nor thieves, nor covetous, nor drunkards, nor revilers, nor extortioners, shall inherit the kingdom of God.* **11** *And such were some of you: but ye are washed, but ye are sanctified, but ye are justified in the name of the Lord Jesus, and by the Spirit of our God.*

---

92   Ephesians 2:8-9
93   James 2:14-18

This passage seems to be saying that certain sins will keep you out of heaven. A person might be tempted to look at this list, or any other, and say "Whew, I'm not guilty of any of those so I can relax. I don't have to worry that I am not saved." If we analyze this verse carefully we'll find that it is harder than we might think to stay off of it. Look at the list:

1. <u>Fornicators</u> – Fornication is sexual intercourse between two people who are not married. That was one of the sins that David committed and we know that David will be in heaven.

2. <u>Idolaters</u> – This one of the sins that it is possible to be guilty of and not even be aware that it is being committed. At times we place the importance of worldly items above God. The Greek word for this is *eidololatres* and it means *an image of worship.* It also can mean *literally or figuratively.* It is not necessary to have a graven image, our object of worship can be figurative, as in an activity or something we value.

3. <u>Adulterers</u> – Remember what Jesus taught us about adultery. If we lust in our hearts, we are guilty of this sin[94].

4. <u>Effeminate</u> – This is speaking of homosexuality. This sin is so repulsive to us that we often single it out as one that can't possibly forgiven. As vile as it seems to us, it is a sin like all others. Do we think that God is not able to forgive <u>some</u> sin?

5. <u>Abusers of themselves with mankind</u> – This also is speaking of homosexuality.

6. <u>Thieves</u> – This is a pretty large group. A thief is a thief, whether it be a large sum of money, or a pen from work. (I will admit that if we are not careful we can get pretty legalistic on this one).

7. <u>Covetous</u> – Unless you are handsome (or beautiful),

---

rich, famous, witty, athletic, <u>and</u> popular – there is a good chance you have committed this sin.

8. <u>Drunkards</u>- Which scripture condemns drinking? There is <u>no argument</u> however that getting drunk is a sin[95].

9. <u>Revilers</u> – The Greek word indicates that this is a person who is just plain mean and lives a life that is just plain mean.

10. <u>Extortioners</u> – This means just what it says.

The point here is that it would not be surprising to find yourself on this list somewhere, even <u>after</u> you are a Christian. The truth is that in the real world that Satan roars[96] about in, it is easy to stumble into sin. If everyone on the list had their salvation revoked, hell would be even more crowded than sadly, it will be.

Another look at the above passage and we realize that Paul says "And *such were some of you: but ye are washed, but ye are sanctified, but ye are justified in the name of the Lord Jesus, and by the Spirit of our God*". In other words, those sins are forgiven. Welcome to the world of the mercy and grace of God. What if a person commits those sins after they become a Christian? Does God revoke their salvation? I believe that at this point we revert back to **Romans 11:29**. God does not take His gifts back because of our actions. It only makes sense, because He does not bestow them because of our actions. Remember, salvation is a gift, and we obtain the gift by faith.

Make no mistake, we are being admonished that these sins are repulsive (as is all sin). A Christian has an obligation to avoid sin at all time. We know that is not possible, but still it is our goal. Our motivation for attempting to be sin free should be our love of God and our sincere desire to do His will, not our fear that we will go to hell.

Does this mean that everyone who calls themselves a

95   Romans 13:13; Ephesians 5:18
96   1 Peter 5:8

Christian is one? It does not. **Matthew 7:21** answers this very clearly: ***Not every one that saith unto me, Lord, Lord, shall enter into the kingdom of heaven; but he that doeth the will of my Father which is in heaven***. What is the "*will of my Father which is in heaven*"? His will is that we should trust in Jesus for salvation. This scripture means that it is not enough to mouth the words like a puppet, but a person has to mean it when they pray the prayer of salvation. **Colossians 2:14** assures us that our sins are forgiven and they are forgotten once we truly accept Christ as Savior. The last passage of scripture that I want to include on this subject is: **Galatians 3:22** *But the scripture hath concluded all under sin, that the promise by faith of Jesus Christ might be given to them that believe.**23** But before faith came, we were kept under the law, shut up unto the faith which should afterwards be revealed.* **24** *Wherefore the law was our schoolmaster to bring us unto Christ, that we might be justified by faith.*

The Word of God is telling us that yes, there was a time when our actions were what got us into heaven, (looking towards the cross). Those days are gone. Since Jesus Christ died on the cross for our sins we are under grace. We are saved through faith.

I believe that it is clear that we can not win - and we can not lose – our salvation <u>by our actions.</u>

Chapter Nineteen

What Does it Mean?

Every kid used to sing the alphabet song in the first grade or in kindergarten. I used to like to sing it because it meant I totally knew my ABCs. There was one part I didn't understand. I could not figure out why they threw in "L-M-N-O-P". I didn't realize they were individual letters. I thought that, right in the middle of the song, we were singing "elemennopee". Who knew why? I was a senior in high school before I figured it out.

I do think it is possible to be a *senior* in Christianity and <u>not</u> understand some scriptures. It happens to me all of the time and I'm a sophomore Christian. As you read this, you might think I'm talking about prophecy from Revelation or Daniel. I'm not. I'm speaking about verses that we might have a tendency to skip over, or to allow someone to interpret for us – falsely.

The reason I wanted to do this chapter is three fold. It is a good way to point out the way some people can take a verse and miss-interpret it. In fact, there are many times they do it on purpose. The second reason is that it is a good chance to learn more about how to study the Bible. The third reason is because I think it will be kind of fun. Let's get started with an easy passage.

RICH PEOPLE AND HEAVEN

Matthew 19:23 *Then said Jesus unto his disciples, Verily I say unto you, That a rich man shall hardly enter into the kingdom of heaven.* **24** *And again I say unto you, It is easier for a camel to go through the eye of a needle, than for a rich man to enter into the kingdom of God.*

When we read this verse it seems pretty clear. It says it's easier for a camel to go through the eye of a needle than it is for a rich man to go to heaven. Doesn't that mean that rich people can not get to heaven? After all, when we say things like that, we mean it is <u>not</u> going to happen. For example, when we say "I'll wear a tie when pigs fly" we are really saying, "I'll never wear a tie". So isn't Jesus really saying that rich people go to hell? Let's see. Go down to the next two verses for the answer:

Matthew 19:25 *When his disciples heard it, they were exceedingly amazed, saying, Who then can be saved?* **26** *But Jesus beheld them, and said unto them, With men this is impossible; but with God all things are possible.*

We don't have to feel bad, the disciples didn't get it either. Jesus is telling us that yes, it is impossible for a camel to go through the eye of a needle - for men. For God it is possible, and in fact with God it would be nothing. So what is Jesus saying? He is telling us that sometimes our worldly desires can make it extremely difficult for us to come to Christ. It might be our money; it might be a desire for something else. These things can all be overcome – **if** – God is working, and we are being drawn by Him. From a Bible study perspective, the other lesson here is that sometimes we have to read the verses before and/or after the text to get the full meaning.

SNAKE HANDLING

Mark 16:16 *He that believeth and is baptized shall be saved; but he that believeth not shall be damned.* **17** *And these signs shall follow them that believe; In my name shall they cast out devils; they shall speak with new tongues;* **18** *They shall take up serpents; and if they drink any deadly thing, it shall not hurt them; they shall lay hands on the sick, and they shall recover.*

This passage is responsible for the early demise of quite a few folks[97]. You might ask, "In some churches they handle snakes. Sometimes they get bit and die. Is it because they don't have enough faith? I mean, it very clearly states that '*They shall take up serpents; and if they drink any deadly thing, it shall not hurt them*'". This is a classic example of someone taking a passage and making a whole doctrine out of it – that is 100% **incorrect**. Let's look.

> **Note:** I probably shouldn't do this, but I can't help it. I wanted to put a few things in here about modern snake handlers so you could get realistic view of these people. There is a part of me that wants to call them idiots but, in the words of *Fox News*, "I'll report – you decide". The modern snake handler cult was founded by George Went Hensley. He was born around 1880, although his exact date of birth is unknown. His exact date of death is known, July 25, 1955. So is his exact <u>cause</u> of death – snakebite[98]. Snake Handlers are more generally known as the Church of God with Signs Following. An exact number is unknown due to the autonomy of

---

97   Also Luke 10:19
98   Kimborough 1995, 133;

each individual group. Estimates range between 1,000 and 2,000 total church members[99]. There are numerous documented deaths by snakebite.

Back to the Bible. Why did Jesus say what he did? Even if you read the verses before and after this passage, it doesn't change anything. The words are the same. In fact, these instructions are also given elsewhere in the Bible[100]. So what is our explanation?

John 4:48 *Then said Jesus unto him, Except ye see signs and wonders, ye will not believe.*

Why did Jesus perform miracles? He performed miracles to authenticate the fact that He was indeed the Son of God. The miracles that Jesus performed are known as "sign miracles". He did not do them to show off or to bribe people. There had been many who came before Him, claiming to be the Messiah. There will be many who will come after Him in an attempt to deceive.

Matthew 24:5 *For many shall come in my name, saying, I am Christ; and shall deceive many.*

Note: Historically we know that some of the false saviors that came before Jesus had hundreds, and sometimes thousands of followers. Since the crucifixion and resurrection of Christ there have been other false Messiahs. Where are they now? The answer is simple. They died and they **stayed** dead. A couple of them probably died from a rattlesnake bite.

Back to the subject. Imagine yourself in the world back

99 Nation wide according to Barnhill & Davis, *cults and others*
100 Luke 10:19

in the days before Jesus. All of a sudden, you begin to hear rumors. Supposedly, there is a man who claims he is the Son of God. You think to yourself, "Here we go again, another one of these false prophets". Then one day you happen to see this *man*. You see Him heal the sick and raise the dead. No camera tricks. No one is turned away because they are too withered, too sick or too dead. He takes care of ALL of them. Wouldn't you be a lot more likely to think to yourself, "There is something to this"? Our God of infinite wisdom knew this - and that was the reason Jesus performed these miracles on the earth.

Although Christ returned to heaven, there was still work for His followers. Many had not heard about Jesus. In order for these new missionaries to be effective, God gave them the ability to perform "sign miracles". We no longer have this ability. If you doubt this, don't go pick up a snake. Instead, pick up your Bible[101].

Matthew 16:4 *A wicked and adulterous generation seeketh after a sign; and there shall no sign be given unto it, but the sign of the prophet Jonas. And he left them, and departed.*

Why doesn't God give us signs today? Does He give us anything instead? The answer is yes. He gives us the Bible <u>and</u> He gives us the Holy Spirit*102*.

John 14:16 *And I will pray the Father, and he shall give you another Comforter, that he may abide with you for ever;*

Remember that the Bible is the <u>Word of God</u>[103] and that it is often referred to as the <u>sword of the Spirit</u>[104].

---

101   Also: Mark 8:12;Matthew 12:39;
102   John 14:26; John 15:26; Acts 2:38; John 16:7-14
103   Romans 10:17; Colossians 1:25 & 26; 1 Thessalonians 2:13; Hebrews 4:12; Revelation 3:8
104   Also read Luke 8:5-11 and note what verse 11 says about the seed

Ephesians 6:17 *And take the helmet of salvation, and the sword of the Spirit, which is the word of God:*

We have the Bible. In Jesus' time they had no book which combined the entire body of scriptures, much less one that was available to everyone. Don't forget, there was no New Testament available to them. Today we have the Word of God. We also have the Holy Spirit. We do not have the gift of <u>sign</u> miracles. Make no mistake. God still performs miracles – but that is another subject.

SALVATION BY WORKS?

James 2:20 *But wilt thou know, O vain man, that faith without works is dead?*

James 2:21 *Was not Abraham our father justified by works, when he had offered Isaac his son upon the altar?*

James 2:26 *For as the body without the spirit is dead, so faith without works is dead also.*

James 2:14 *What doth it profit, my brethren, though a man say he hath faith, and have not works? can faith save him?*

These verses out of the Book of James teach us a great lesson. You can take specific verses out of the Bible, show them to someone who is not familiar with the Gospel, and convince him or her of just about anything. In fact, it is being done every day. Whole churches are springing up based upon false scriptural doctrine. Jesus told us this was going to happen.

Acts 20:29 *For I know this, that after my departing shall grievous wolves enter in among you, not sparing the flock.* **30** *Also of your own selves shall men arise, speaking perverse things, to draw away disciples after them.*

So what do these passages mean? It sure looks like we need works in order to be saved. After all, **James 2:14** even asks the question *"can faith save him?"* Passages like these require a little detective work. How would we begin to reconcile something like this? Let's look at the steps:

Step one: <u>Look at what we know to be true</u>. As Christians we know that we are saved by grace – not by works**. (Ephesians 2: 8** *For by grace are ye saved through faith; and that not of yourselves: it is the gift of God*)[105]

Step two: <u>Realize that the Bible does not contradict itself</u>. If the Bible contradicted itself that would be evidence that it was not 100% true. As Christians we know that it <u>is</u> true because it is the infallible, inspired Word of God. (**2 Timothy 3:16** *All scripture is given by inspiration of God, and is profitable for doctrine, for reproof, for correction, for instruction in righteousness:*)

Step three: <u>When something seems to contradict in the Bible – fall back on faith and seek the answer</u>. (**Ephesians 6:16** *Above all, taking the shield of faith, wherewith ye shall be able to quench all the fiery darts of the wicked.*) This is a wonderful verse that we overlook sometimes. When those *"fiery darts"* are coming our way we may not have the correct answer. In that case we need to take up our shield of faith and hold it up until we can figure out what is going on. In this case, we are trusting that God's word will help us figure out the apparent discrepancy between works and faith.

Step four: <u>Search the Bible for the answer.</u> Don't hesitate to get help. I want you to know that there is not a week that goes by that I don't have a question for Pastor Ken or Pastor Chris. I would not hesitate to go to one of our Deacons with a question. I encourage you to do the same. There is other help

---

105   **Ephesians 2: 9** *Not of works, lest any man should boast.*

available as well. Every church has many men and women in the congregation who are Bible scholars. You shouldn't hesitate to call on any of them. Sometimes a good discussion is beneficial. Don't forget about Bible study tools like commentaries, Bible dictionaries, and a good concordance. There is also a lot of valuable help on line. Remember to be careful to pick and choose so that you are not led astray by some hack.

Let's use the steps listed above to solve our mystery. Step One says to take a look at what we **know** to be true. We know that we are saved by grace. That means we can rule out being saved by works. Step two is automatic. We know the Bible does not contradict. Step three tells us to fall back on our faith. Let's do that and go to step four. Let's search the Bible for the answer. That's the fun part anyway. Start by reading the entire second chapter of James. The point will be clear. James is saying that now that you are saved, how about letting us see it. **James 2:14** is referring to someone who asks a Christian for help. James is asking, what in the world good does it do to tell a brother in need that you have faith – if – you have no works to go along with it?

We were recently visited by the a missionary family who are missionaries to Papua New Guinea. We support them with prayer and with money. They have got to have financial support in order to carry on their work. Imagine if we would have told them, "We think you are doing fine work. We are Christians. Don't worry about a thing; after all, we have faith. Bye." What good would that have done them, or more specifically – what good would that have done God? They need money! That requires *works* on someone's part. On the other hand, our willingness to support them (our works) does not save us. Rather, it is our faith that is the foundation that motivates us to perform these works.

TURN THE OTHER CHEEK?

Matthew 5:39 *But I say unto you, That ye resist not evil: but* *whosoever shall smite thee on thy right cheek, turn to him the other also.*

This verse has been misunderstood as much as any verse in the Bible. Does it mean that you should stand by and let someone beat you to a pulp? It very clearly states that we should not resist. It obviously says to turn the other cheek. Let's investigate. In this passage Jesus is teaching us the way that Christians should act. Please allow me to use something that happened to me to illustrate what I believe this passage means.

When my daughter was a little girl I got roped into coaching her softball team. I was probably the most unqualified coach who ever lived, but I did my best. I had a pretty strict policy that parents could not scream at their kids and that the top priorities of our team was to learn the basics, and to have fun. Some of the parents thought that my top priority for these little girls should have been to win. At one of our games, unbeknownst to me, one of the fathers was setting in the stands working himself into frenzy because his daughter was not pitching, and we were losing. When he could no longer stand it he jumped down from the stands, and in front of about fifty people, he attacked me and began to scream at me. He was a real small fellow and very out of shape and weak, (fortunately for me). He bumped his chest against mine and I did not respond physically. He did it again and I did not retaliate. He head- butted me and I told him he was acting like a maniac and he should stop because the girls (including my daughter) were crying. He slapped me and I told him I had just about had it with him. He hit me in the jaw with his fist and I defended myself.

Here is the point. By the grace of God I managed to keep my Christian witness that day. No one who saw me would have been surprised to learn that I am a Christian, even though I ended up hitting this guy. Although there were many times I had failed to do it in the past, I had turned the other cheek that day. Please stay with me because there are a couple of important points here. I did not feel like I was in danger from this guy. I did not think he was going to kill me or hurt my family. Had I felt that way, I would have had a different obligation as a Christian. I would have had to do whatever was in my power to stop him immediately. Would this have caused me to lose my Christian witness? I don't believe so.

Here is the bottom line on this verse. Don't be so quick to act like a heathen. It (literally) does not kill us sometimes to walk away from a verbal or a physical confrontation. Sometimes we pride ourselves on the fact that "I don't take nothing off of nobody". Turning the other cheek can be difficult, even in a verbal assault. Sometimes it is the scriptural thing to do. By no means do I believe that we should put ourselves or our family in harms way and use this verse as an excuse. Once again, this is an example of a time when we can call on the common sense that God has given to us.

Do Not Eat Pigs?

Deuteronomy 14:8 *And the swine, because it divideth the hoof, yet cheweth not the cud, it is unclean unto you: ye shall not eat of their flesh, nor touch their dead carcase.*

Believe it or not, there are a lot of folks out there who are convinced that it is a sin to eat pork. I was watching one of the television Bible teachers a couple of weeks ago and he quoted Old Testament scriptures that forbid eating certain foods. He then went on to explain that they were (and are) forbidden. This is a fellow who knows the Bible. Let's see if we can figure out if this teacher was correct or not.

The verse that is listed above is part of the Old Testament Law that was given to Moses. The question is, since it is in the Bible, and it is a rule, don't we have to obey it? We've already established that one of the purposes of the Bible is to provide *"instruction in righteousness".106*

106   2 Timothy 3:16

> **Note:** I want to say right up front that I do not know for <u>absolute certain</u> why God gave specific instructions concerning food. I have read and heard a lot of theories that I think make good sense. Most of the theories involve health. In those days there were concerns that are not an issue today. We have refrigeration, proper processing procedures and numerous other ways to keep pork and other meats from going bad. They didn't. The bottom line is this – it is not a show stopper for me that I don't know the exact reason God put some food off limits. I just know that He did.

If it was wrong to eat certain foods back then (and it was), why isn't it wrong now? This is another example of why we've got to be willing to look at the whole Bible in order to come to the correct conclusion. Check out the following passage.[107]

Romans 14: 14 *I know, and am persuaded by the Lord Jesus, that there is nothing unclean of itself: but to him that esteemeth any thing to be unclean, to him it is unclean.* **15** *But if thy brother be grieved with thy meat, now walkest thou not charitably. Destroy not him with thy meat, for whom Christ died.*

This seems pretty easy to me. I doubt if I would have included this passage if I hadn't seen the guy on TV talking about it. He represents a large group of believers who are convinced they should not eat pork. The fellow I'm talking about is very knowledgeable. It's a mystery to me that he can feel the way he does.

ARE WE ALL A BUNCH OF MURDERERS AND ADULTERERS?

Matthew 5:21 *Ye have heard that it was said by them of old*

107   Also Acts 10:12-15

time, Thou shalt not kill; and whosoever shall kill shall be in danger of the judgment: **22** *But I say unto you, That whosoever is angry with his brother without a cause shall be in danger of the judgment: and whosoever shall say to his brother, Raca108, shall be in danger of the council: but whosoever shall say, Thou fool, shall be in danger of hell fire.*

Matthew 5:27 *Ye have heard that it was said by them of old time, Thou shalt not commit adultery:* **28** *But I say unto you, That whosoever looketh on a woman to lust after her hath committed adultery with her already in his heart.*

These are a couple of passages that might cause you to take a second glance. Is Jesus saying that if you hate someone – you are a murderer? And is He saying that if you lust after someone, you are an adulterer? Let's see if we can come to a conclusion. Once again Jesus is addressing the issue of <u>works</u>.

Matthew 5:20 *For I say unto you, That except your righteousness shall exceed the righteousness of the scribes and Pharisees, ye shall in no case enter into the kingdom of heaven.*

In **Matthew 5:20** Jesus is saying that unless you are so good that " *your righteousness shall exceed the righteousness of the scribes and Pharisees,*" you are on your way to hell. What does that mean? Jesus is telling us that the Pharisees were about as close to perfection (in following the rules) as you can get. However, (and this is a giant however), they are still not good enough to get into heaven based on their works. Then, just in case there were some folks who still didn't get the idea, He went a little further into His explanation. He told us that if you are feeling pretty good because you obey the Ten Commandments, think again. Here is where it gets a little tricky.

---

108   Strong's Ref. # 4469 of Aramaic origin; a term of utter vilification

When I was a cop I arrested people for murder, and I arrested them for attempted murder. I always wondered why attempted murder carries a lighter sentence than murder. It is almost like we are rewarding someone for being too incompetent to commit the crime they wanted to commit. Let me relate that to what Jesus is saying. Imagine that I hated John Doe. Imagine that I hated him so much that if the opportunity arose I would kill him. Imagine that if I could say a word and John Doe would die – I <u>would</u> say that word. In fact, the only reason I do not kill him is because I am afraid of him, or am afraid I will get caught. In my heart I want him murdered. My heart is what convicts me. My heart is what makes me guilty.

I'd be surprised if there were not some people in the world who you don't like. There have probably been times when you would have used the word hate to describe how you felt about someone. The question is, would you have murdered them if you could have? I believe that Jesus is saying that just because the opportunity did not present it's self, don't think you are any less guilty than the person who had the chance and took it. The same applies for adultery. It is one thing to look at a person and think they are attractive. It is quite another to look at them and know in your heart that if you had the chance – you would have an affair with them. At any rate Jesus was telling us not to put too much faith in our own ability to be good, because we are not nearly as good as we might think that we are. I believe that Jesus said exactly what He meant. If we lust after someone, or if we hate someone enough to kill them, we are guilty of the crime.

CAN I HAVE ANYTHING I WANT?

Matthew 7:7 *Ask, and it shall be given you; seek, and ye shall find; knock, and it shall be opened unto you:*

Wow, what a concept. All you have to do is ask God for something and He'll give it to you. So, if I want a new Dodge Durango all I have to do is to pray for it, and maybe get some of you to pray with me, and God will deliver it? Isn't that what the scripture is saying? Let's go back to the analogy we often use, the human parent and child. For my example I'll go back to my Granddad. I always knew that he would do anything for me that he could. I knew because he did, and because he told me that he would. Once, when I was a teenager, I wanted him to give me a ride to the edge of town so that I could hitch hike to another town about 150 miles away. (I know it sounds stupid now, but in those days and in that location we did it all the time.) My granddad would not do it. He told me that hitchhiking was dangerous and that on top of that there was a law against it. So – he did not give me a ride.

I knew even then that it bothered my granddad a lot more than it did me. He loved me, and he wanted to do anything he could for me. My granddad knew a lot more about what was good for me than I did. Even though he told me that he would do anything for me, there were times when he turned me down. My parents were the same way. I grew up knowing that they would do anything for me. My dad could have afforded to buy me a motorcycle. I really wanted one. He told me no. He told me that a kid my age, and as reckless as I was, had no business with one. Now of course I know he was right.

We ask God for things that He could easily "afford" to give us. God is so much wiser than us. He knows when to say no. I did not understand why I couldn't have a motorcycle. I do now. I don't understand why God says no when we ask for things that mean so much to us. I just know that He does. It should not cause us to quit trusting Him. It should not cause us to quit believing the Bible is true. It should make us realize all the more that God is in control, and we need to realize that our wisdom is nowhere equal to His.

One of the reasons that I wanted to put this particular

passage into this chapter is because a lot of television preachers throw scriptures like this at us and tell us that all we have to do is ask for something, (and send them some money). Not only is God in total control – but – we can go straight to Him with our requests. We don't need to pay anyone, send in money as a token of our faith, or anything else. God is my Father, and He is your Father. We should go to Him with all our requests[109] and all our concerns[110]. We should go to Him in complete faith[111], realizing that He is in control, and knowing that He will do what is best – whether we understand it (and agree with it) or not.

Bottom Line

There are a lot of passages in the Bible that can be difficult. Some of them have been falsely interpreted in order to make someone rich. Others have been incorrectly interpreted by good people who love the Lord but didn't take the time to figure out what God was actually saying. Do not let anyone (including me) lead you astray. Seek the truth in, and through scripture. Watch out for someone asking you for money in order for them to pray for you. Also, someone asking for money and telling you that God will not believe you have faith unless you give. (<u>Do not use this as an excuse not to tithe</u>.)

You have a church family. You have a Pastor. You have Deacons. You have a whole body of folks who love you. You do not have to send a piece of cloth to anyone. You don't have to get someone to send you some water that they got out of the river Jordon. You have everything you need right here – and it is free.

---

109   1 Thessalonians 5:17; Matthew 21:22
110   Philippians 4:6
111   <u>Just a very few scriptures of the many on faith</u>: Matthew 6:30; Matthew 9:22; Matthew 14:31; Mark 4:40; Mark 11:22;

Chapter Twenty
The Holy Spirit

The purpose of this chapter is to take an in-depth look at the Holy Spirit. The intent is to walk away with a real understanding of exactly who the Holy Spirit is - and how He affects us as Christians.

My Pastor has an excellent analogy of the Holy Spirit and an egg. An egg is composed of three parts, the shell, the white, and the yoke. The shell is egg, the white is egg, and the yoke is egg. Even though it is composed of three parts - it is still just <u>one</u> egg.

That comparison is useful when we try to understand the Holy Trinity of God. We have God the Father, God the Son, and God the Holy Spirit. Even though all three are God - there is still just one God. That is a difficult concept to understand, and it helps to know the intent of each.

God the Father made us. He loves us and protects us. He governs the world and guides us in all we do. God has a love for us that is beyond any comprehension. In fact, He loved us so much that he sent his Son, Jesus into the world to die for our sins. Jesus lived his life on this earth 100% man and 100% God. Again, that is a difficult concept to understand. Jesus came to earth to die for our sins. He was crucified, buried and resurrected. We know that once we exercise our faith in the

Lord and truly accept this free gift in our hearts, we are saved and are heaven bound.

The problem is we can not have this initial <u>or</u> long-lasting faith by ourselves. God in His wisdom sent us help in the form of the Holy Spirit. The Holy Spirit guides us, helps us with scriptural interpretation, and <u>convicts us of our sins</u>. Every Christian has the Holy Spirit living in them. The point we ignore though is this: Unless we <u>allow</u> the Holy Spirit to work in our lives - we can not and will not be successful in our quest to live more Christ-like lives.

The Greek Word (Holy **Ghost**)

1. **pneu'ma** - the third person of the triune God, the Holy Spirit, coequal, co-eternal with the Father and the Son
   a. sometimes referred to in a way which emphasizes his personality and character (the \\Holy\\ Spirit)
   b. sometimes referred to in a way which emphasizes his work and power (the Spirit of \\Truth\\)
   c. never referred to as a depersonalized force
      1. the spiritual nature of Christ, higher than the highest angels and equal to God, the divine nature of Christ

HAS THE HOLY SPIRIT ALWAYS BEEN AVAILABLE TO EVERYONE?

In Old Testament times the Holy Spirit did not abide in humans like He does today. The **Old Testament** tells us the Holy Spirit came upon people, anointing them for a **specific** task or purpose:

Exodus 31: *1. And the Lord spake unto Moses, saying, 2. See, I have called by name Bezaleel the son of Uri, the son of Hur, of the tribe of Judah: 3. And I have filled him with the spirit of God, in wisdom, and in understanding, and in knowledge, and in all manner of workmanship, 4. To devise cunning works, to work* *in gold, and in silver, and in brass,* **5.** *And in cutting of stones, to set them, and in carving of timber, to work in all manner of workmanship.*

Numbers 24: 2. *And Balaam lifted up his eyes, and he saw Israel abiding in his tents according to their tribes; and the spirit of God came upon him.*

During the time Jesus walked the earth the Holy Spirit did not in-dwell individuals either. Again – the Holy Spirit came upon individuals in order for them to do God's work. It was not until Jesus had already ascended into heaven, on the day of Pentecost that the gift of the Holy Spirit came to earth to minister to us full time.

Jesus told His disciples not to leave Jerusalem until they received the "promise of the Father", the Holy Spirit. **Acts 1:4**. *And, being assembled together with them, commanded them that they should not depart from Jerusalem, but wait for the promise of the Father, which, saith he, ye have heard of me.* **5.** *For John truly baptized with water; but ye shall be baptized with the Holy Ghost not many days hence.* Even though the Disciples had walked with Jesus and observed His miracles and His manner of teaching, Jesus knew they were not prepared – or able – to continue the ministry alone.

Acts 2: 1. *And when the day of Pentecost was fully come, they were all with one accord in one place.* **2.** *And suddenly there came a sound from heaven as of a rushing mighty wind, and it filled all the house where they were sitting.* **3.** *And there appeared unto them cloven tongues like as of fire, and it sat upon each of them.* **4.** *And they were all filled with the Holy Ghost, and began to speak with other tongues, as the Spirit gave them utterance.* **5.** *And there were dwelling at Jerusalem Jews, devout men, out of every nation under heaven.* **6.** *Now when this was noised abroad, the multitude came together, and were confounded, because that every man heard them speak in his own language.*

7. *And they were all amazed and marvelled, saying one to another, Behold, are not all these which speak Galilaeans?* **8.** *And how hear we every man in our own tongue, wherein we were born?* **9.** *Parthians, and Medes, and Elamites, and the dwellers in Mesopotamia, and in Judaea, and Cappadocia, in Pontus, and Asia,*

10. *Phrygia, and Pamphylia, in Egypt, and in the parts of Libya about Cyrene, and strangers of Rome, Jews and proselytes,* **11.** *Cretes and Arabians, we do hear them speak in our tongues the wonderful works of God.* **12.** *And they were all amazed, and were in doubt, saying one to another, What meaneth this?*

The folks who witnessed this event were afraid, and accused the persons involved of being drunk with wine. That is when Peter stood up and preached to them.

Acts 2: 14. *But Peter, standing up with the eleven, lifted up his voice, and said unto them, Ye men of Judaea, and all ye that dwell at Jerusalem, be this known unto you, and hearken to my words:* **15.** *For these are not drunken, as ye suppose, seeing it is but the third hour of the day.* **16.** *But this is that which was spoken by the prophet Joel;*

17. *And it shall come to pass in the last days, saith God, I will pour out of my Spirit upon all flesh: and your sons and your daughters shall prophesy, and your young men shall see visions, and your old men shall dream dreams:*

18. *And on my servants and on my handmaidens I will pour out in those days of my Spirit; and they shall prophesy:*

Peter went on, full of the Holy Spirit to very bravely tell these people about Jesus. These were the very ones who had screamed for Jesus' blood a few weeks earlier. (**Acts 2:23.** *Him, being delivered by the determinate counsel and foreknowledge* *of God, ye have taken, and by wicked hands have crucified and slain*) Peter preached to them, and accused them. As a result of the work of the Holy Spirit these (3000 (+/-) people were saved.

Acts 2: 38. *Then Peter said unto them, Repent, and be baptized every one of you in the name of Jesus Christ for the remission of sins, and ye shall receive the gift of the Holy Ghost.* **39.** *For the promise is unto you, and to your children, and to all that are afar off, even as many as the Lord our God shall call.* **40.** *And with many other words did he testify and exhort, saying, Save yourselves from this untoward generation.* **41.** *Then they that gladly received his word were baptized: and the same day there were added unto them about three thousand souls.*

From that moment on everyone who accepted Christ as their Savior received the Holy Spirit as a companion in their Christian walk.

IS THE HOLY SPIRIT A PERSON OR A FORCE?112

The Bible teaches that the Holy Spirit is a Person. In John chapters 14, 15, and 16, for example, Jesus spoke of the Holy Spirit as "He" because He has all the attributes of personality and is not merely an impersonal force. Jesus also referred to the Holy Spirit as the <u>Comforter or the Counselor</u> (**John 14:16** *And I will pray the Father, and he shall give you another Comforter, that he may abide with you for ever;*) (**John 15: 26.** *But when the Comforter is come, whom I will send unto you from the Father, even the Spirit of truth, which proceedeth from the Father, he shall testify of me:*) This title conveys the ideas of advising, exhorting, comforting, strengthening, interceding, and encouraging.

In addition, the Bible makes it clear that the Holy Spirit is

---

112   ffDecision Magazine Weekly Devotional; February 2002 (Billy Graham)

God Himself. In **Acts 5: 1-4** a man who lied to the Holy Spirit is said to have lied to God. The Holy Spirit also is described in the Bible as having the characteristics of God and doing God's work. He convicts people of sin, righteousness, and judgment (John 16: **8**. *And when he is come, he will reprove the world of sin, and of righteousness, and of judgment:* **9**. *Of sin, because they believe not on me;* **10.** *Of righteousness, because I go to my Father, and ye see me no more;* 11. *Of judgment, because the prince of this world is judged.*) and gives new life to those who trust in Jesus (**John 3:8**). That He is the third Person of the Holy Trinity is made clear by His inclusion with the Father and the Son in such Bible passages as (Matthew 28:19 *Go ye therefore, and teach all nations, baptizing them in the name of the Father, and of the Son, and of the Holy Ghost:*).

In the **New Testament**, the Holy Spirit dwells within all believers (1 Corinthians 6:**19** *What? know ye not that your body is the temple of the Holy Ghost which is in you, which ye have of God, and ye are not your own?*) and assures them that they are children of God (Romans 8:16 *The Spirit itself beareth witness with our spirit, that we are the children of God:*). (**Romans 8: 9**: *But ye are not in the flesh, but in the Spirit, if so be that the Spirit of God dwell in you. Now if any man have not the Spirit of Christ, he is none of his.* **15** *For ye have not received the spirit of bondage again to fear; but ye have received the Spirit of adoption, whereby we cry, Abba, Father.*)

IF THE HOLY SPIRIT IN-DWELLS IN EVERY TRUE CHRISTIAN – WHY AREN'T WE ALL 100% COMMITTED TO THE LORD?

He Can Be Resisted: **Acts 7:51** *Ye stiffnecked and uncircumcised in heart and ears, ye do always resist the Holy Ghost: as your fathers did, so do ye.*

2 Corinthians 3: 17 *Now the Lord is that Spirit: and where the Spirit of the Lord is, there is liberty.*

We have discussed in this book the fact that God did not make a bunch of robots, who walk around blindly obeying an unseen force with no power to disobey. God gave us free will. As great a gift as the Holy Spirit is, He is only as effective as we allow Him to be. We do have the authority to "not listen" if we choose.

The Holy Spirit and the Church

After the death and resurrection of Jesus, the Disciples obviously had a much greater faith than before. When we consider all of the obstacles they would have to overcome, (hatred, disbelief, etc.), from the very people who had just crucified Christ, it is not hard to understand why they needed some serious help. The fact is – so do we. Any Church, including yours, that is not Holy Spirit led, is doomed to failure. Paul told the church at Ephesus:

Ephesians 1: *In whom ye also trusted, after that ye heard the word of truth, the gospel of your salvation: in whom also after that ye believed, ye were sealed with that holy Spirit of promise,* **14.** *Which is the earnest of our inheritance until the redemption of the purchased possession, unto the praise of his glory.* **15.** *Wherefore I also, after I heard of your faith in the Lord Jesus, and love unto all the saints,* **16.** *Cease not to give thanks for you, making mention of you in my prayers;* **17.** *That the God of our Lord Jesus Christ, the Father of glory, may give unto you the spirit of wisdom and revelation in the knowledge of him:* **18.** *The eyes of your understanding being enlightened; that ye may know what is the hope of his calling, and what the riches of the glory of his inheritance in the saints,* **19.** *And what is the exceeding greatness* *of his power to us-ward who believe, according to the working of his mighty power,*

The truth is that yes, a church **can** continue to grow in numbers based solely on individual talents. The largest church in the state can be the largest because the Pastor is flamboyant, or because the music director is so talented. A congregation can leave the Holy Spirit completely out of their ministry. God will allow this to happen. But – there are signs. Is God's will being done? Are people being saved? Are people being allowed to join the church just for the sake of growth, without any interest or follow-up to insure they really understand the plan of salvation? Are people being healed because of scriptural Christian prayer? Is the word of God being taught regardless of the consequences? Is the Pastor a Godly man who lives the life he preaches? Are the Deacons Godly men who truly care about the congregation, or simply the most popular or influential? Are there hard feelings and jealousies among members? Do we put our own individual triumphs first – not giving God the glory?

I think you should all ask this question about your Church. Is it a Church that believes in the power of prayer? Are you in a church that believes in scripture? Have you seen miracles performed in your church in the form of scriptural healing, persons saved, strength granted, and on and on? The Holy Spirit should lead your church, and as long as you continue to pray and ask for guidance, always seeking the true will of God, you will be successful.

I feel like I need to stop here and clarify a couple of points:

1. We **have** had folks healed, and other miracles in our congregation. We have not seen the kind of flashy, "look at me" type healing that we see on television. We have seen true scriptural healing, based on the

> power of the prayers of good Christians in our church, praying for and believing in a common goal.

2. Our success will be measured with God's measuring stick, not ours. The size of a church, big or small, is not an indication of whether or not God's will is being done.

Revelation 2: 17 - *He that hath an ear, let him hear what the Spirit saith unto the churches...*

WHAT ELSE DOES THE HOLY SPIRIT DO?

<u>He Teaches:</u> **John 14:26**: *But the Comforter, which is the Holy Ghost, whom the Father will send in my name, he shall teach you all things, and bring all things to your remembrance, whatsoever I have said unto you.*

It is my belief that we can not advance in our understanding of scripture unless we are led and taught by the Holy Spirit. Before we study the Bible we should ask God to grant us the gift of understanding and assistance – through the teaching of the Holy Spirit. One school teacher in our Sunday school class told us that a teacher can not teach a student who sets back and expects the teacher to do all of the work.

1 Corinthians 2: 13. *Which things also we speak, not in the words which man's wisdom teacheth, but which the Holy Ghost teacheth; comparing spiritual things with spiritual.*

Ephesians 1: 16. *Cease not to give thanks for you, making mention of you in my prayers;* **17.** *That the God of our Lord Jesus Christ, the Father of glory, may give unto you the spirit of wisdom and revelation in the knowledge of him:*

THAT IS PAUL PRAYING FOR THE CHURCH THAT THEY MIGHT HAVE WISDOM THRU THE HOLY SPIRIT.

<u>He speaks</u>: **Acts 1:16** *Men and brethren, this scripture must needs have been fulfilled, which the Holy Ghost by the mouth of David spake before concerning Judas, which was guide to them that took Jesus.*

<u>He Prays:</u> **Romans 8: 26** *Likewise the Spirit also helpeth our infirmities: for we know not what we should pray for as we ought: but the Spirit itself maketh intercession for us with groanings which cannot be uttered.* **27** *And he that searcheth the hearts knoweth what is the mind of the Spirit, because he maketh intercession for the saints according to the will of God.*

We know that we are not always wise enough to know exactly how we should pray in certain circumstances. At times like these we may depend on the Holy Spirit to intercede for us.

<u>He Works Miracles</u>: **Acts 2:4** *And they were all filled with the Holy Ghost, and began to speak with other tongues, as the Spirit gave them utterance.* **Acts 8:39** *And when they were come up out of the water, the Spirit of the Lord caught away Philip, that the eunuch saw him no more: and he went on his way rejoicing.*

I know that we will not be aware of all of the miracles that have been performed on our behalf until we get to heaven and can ask. We've seen a lot of healing in our congregation. I can't help but believe that without the intercessory prayer we've had – some of us would not be here today.

<u>He Commands</u>: **Acts 8:29** *Then the Spirit said unto Philip, Go near, and join thyself to this chariot.*

Do you think that the Holy Spirit of God no longer commands us? Could it be that we just aren't listening when those commands are issued? Could it possibly be that we just flat don't care enough to pay attention?

BOTTOM LINE:

The Lord sent the Holy Spirit to us to comfort us and to guide us. While it is true that the Holy Spirit is here to convict us of sin, His presence should be a comfort to all Christians.

As parents we can not understand why our children don't do certain things we <u>encourage</u> them to do – but don't <u>make</u> them do. We make them go to school, and encourage them to put in an extra hour a day studying. We make them go to church, and encourage them to have Christian friends. Since we are wiser and more experienced, it pains us when our children don't always take our advice. We know how much easier and how much better their lives would be.

It is the same with the encouragement the Holy Spirit gives us. Our lives would be so much easier and so much more enriched if we would truly allow the Holy Spirit to work in our lives. As His children we don't always see this – and as a result – we greatly limit the works that we are capable of.

Our prayers and our goal should be to be as open as possible to the will of God, guided by the Holy Spirit.

Chapter Twenty-One
Quit Talking and Start Walking

Every Sunday it's just about the same story in households all over America. Good people getting ready to come to church are worn out by the time they arrive. Fighting with the kids and struggling to get ready while Satan does everything possible to keep us home can really take the wind out of our spiritual sails.

We finally arrive at Church and gradually start getting convicted about the way we are leading our lives. As the two hours a week that we devote to God progress, we start getting convicted. We realize we are not living the way we should. We remember that we did not read our Bibles at all last week. The Pastor tells us for the thousandth time that the church needs help in the nursery – and we feel bad.

By the time the invitation is given we are feeling horrible because the Holy Spirit has convicted us. We are sincerely sorrowful for what we have and have not done. We privately pledge that we will do better next week – and this time we mean it. We'll develop a family devotional, start praying for the folks on the prayer list, and get up fifteen minutes early so we'll have a little time to read the Bible quietly. And our resolve lasts. Sometimes, if we've really been moved, it can last all the way until Tuesday. Then we forget. And Satan has won again.

This chapter is about how we <u>can</u> quit allowing the evil one to be our master. It is for anyone who has a problem with sin – and that is all of us. If you don't have any sin in your life, you should re-think it because you <u>might</u> have a problem with lying.

This chapter is also for those who have been struggling for years. Those who feel they have sunken so low that there is no way out for them. They have tried and tried – but no matter what they do – Satan always wins out in the end.

This chapter is for anyone struggling with a secret sin … A sin that they just can't stop. It's for those who sin and ask for forgiveness for the exact same sin everyday. The ones who – even as they are asking for forgiveness – know in their hearts that they will fall again. This type of sin usually involves an addiction. It might be to alcohol, drugs, sex, a way of life, selfishness, or even addiction to a person.

This chapter is for new Christians who just don't feel like they are living the way they truly want to. Those who want to take that next step but just keep getting pulled back. It's for those who are asking, "Where is this joy that was promised to me when I became a Christian?"

This chapter is for anyone who wants to be as much like Jesus as is ~~humanly~~ spiritually possible. If you are already totally like Jesus – I'm wasting your time. **(1 John 1:10)** I guarantee you – this chapter is definitely for me. Let's take a look at some folks God did change:

The apostle Paul – Saul (later Paul), who went on to write a huge part of the New Testament is one of my favorite persons in the Bible. He didn't start out as an inspiration to Christians. In fact, during part of his life, the only thing Paul hated more than followers of Jesus, was Jesus Himself. He was consumed with hatred for Christians. He even participated in the brutal execution of one of the great pastors of that day – Stephen.

God changed Saul.

<u>*The woman at the well*</u> – John 4:7-26 tells us the story of Jesus, the Son of God, and the Samaritan woman at the well. If the story took place in modern times we'd probably refer to it as Jesus and the woman or man with the horrible reputation. All of the people present would stand around and congratulate themselves for being so good and wonder why in the world Jesus was spending time with the degenerate.

God changed that woman at the well.

NOTE: If you're like me you're thinking, "so you told us a couple of Bible stories that we already knew. So what? What's the point?" The point is that these folks underwent serious change. My guess is that the change they underwent was a lot more radical than what is required in your life. God changed them – He will change us too – <u>if</u> we'll let Him. And if **He** does it – the change will stick.

NOTE: Now - there is no use going any further with the talk about change if you haven't already committed your life to Christ. Before you can expect any help from God you must be saved. That's the easy part. If you have doubts about your salvation please talk to someone in a church that you trust. Your personal decision to accept Christ is much more important to me than <u>anything</u> else you might read in this book.

We often forget that Salvation is not the end of our new life. It is the start. When God forgives us, and totally forgets all of our sin, a process known as sanctification begins. This is the start of the change that our salvation was meant to initiate in our lives.

2 Corinthians 5: 17 - *Therefore if any man be in Christ, he is* *a new creature: old things are passed away; behold, all things are become new.*

Paul is telling us that when we are saved, we are indeed new creatures. The problem is – we can't just continue business as usual and think that we are pleasing God.

Galatians 2:17 - *But if, while we seek to be justified by Christ, we ourselves also are found sinners, is therefore Christ the minister of sin? God forbid.*

We must not develop the attitude that we have carte blanche to sin. How could we have the audacity to believe that Jesus walked this earth as a man, went through untold trials and tribulations, and was crucified so that we could sin all we wanted to and be forgiven?

1 Peter 2:21 - *For even hereunto were ye called: because Christ also suffered for us, leaving us an example, that ye should follow his steps:*

We have an obligation as Christians to try to live our lives as Christ-like as possible. The good news is – God has a system in place to help us.

What is wrong with just going throughout your day and conducting business as usual? Won't you still go to heaven? A person who sincerely fulfills the requirements of salvation is on their way to heaven. I would be awfully worried if I was saved and felt no inclination to live my life in a manner that is in keeping with scriptural instruction. It is my belief that if a person makes no palpable change in their life after salvation, then <u>they</u> should take a good hard look at whether or not they truly are saved. Notice I said that they should take a look. I don't believe it my place to question their salvation. However, all of us have an obligation to present a person in that category with the facts they need so that they can evaluate their decision.

Matthew 7:16 - *Ye shall know them by their fruits. Do men* *gather grapes of thorns, or figs of thistles?* **17** *Even so every good tree bringeth forth good fruit; but a corrupt tree bringeth forth evil fruit.* **18** *A good tree cannot bring forth evil fruit, neither can a corrupt tree bring forth good fruit.* **19** *Every tree that bringeth not forth good fruit is hewn down, and cast into the fire.* **20** *Wherefore by their fruits ye shall know them.*

This doesn't require a whole lot of commentary. All of us need to take a look at the end products of our lives. How do they compare before and after our salvation? If there is no change – there may be a problem. The good news is that God tells us how to correct it.

1 Thessalonians 4: 1 - *Furthermore then we beseech you, brethren, and exhort you by the Lord Jesus, that as ye have received of us how ye ought to walk and to please God, so ye would abound more and more.*

The truth of the matter is that when we start our new lives as Christians it is difficult. If we don't have a background in the church it's even harder. Folks who were interested in our salvation seem to just forget about us after we're saved. As Christians we fall short in the area of discipleship. We overlook the fact that we have a responsibility to mentor new Christians. New Christians mess up all the time – but – so do those who have been saved for years. The longer we are saved – the better we <u>should</u> do. **1 Thessalonians 4:1** is saying we will do better, with time and experience. What are some of the things that we should be doing?   Everything we do should be designed to bring glory to God.

1 Corinthians 10:31 - *Whether therefore ye eat, or drink, or whatsoever ye do, do all to the glory of God.*

If we could just follow this simple doctrine I could stop writing right now. This little rule would be all that would be required to assure that we are in God's will. The problem is that we don't do everything we do for the glory of God. Even things we do for the church we do for our own glory. We worry about making sure that we get credit for our actions or we want to make sure that everyone knows that whatever we are doing is the best. That attitude negates the spiritual joy God has waiting for us.

Colossians 3: 23 *And whatsoever ye do, do it heartily, as to the Lord, and not unto men;*

24 *Knowing that of the Lord ye shall receive the reward of the inheritance: for ye serve the Lord Christ.* **25** *But he that doeth wrong shall receive for the wrong which he hath done: and there is no respect of persons.*

If a person is looking for fire protection – he or she should look somewhere else. If all they are looking for is a chance to make a ten minute public announcement so that they can continue to live, and not have to worry about hell, they are going to have a horrifying surprise when they die. Sometimes that is our fault. We are in such a big hurry to tell people how many folks got saved in our church that we don't follow up to see if they truly understood what was going on.

Philippians 1:6 - *Being confident of this very thing, that he which hath begun a good work in you will perform it until the day of Jesus Christ:*

This verse is a promise that God will continue to work in our lives. The change is going to take time. Little Leslie used to sing a song in front of our church titled "He's still working on me". That song is so true – and He will continue to work on us until we die or until we refuse to let Him. There are some fundamentals that we can not forget.

We have to be specific about what we need to quit doing – and – what we need to start doing in order to be more Christ-like. We have got to be specific and we have got to be honest. We've got to quit making excuses and we've got to quit rationalizing our actions. God doesn't look at us in the morning and say, "Oh, I see he's in a bad mood. I better not mess with him until he gets his coffee." That sounds silly – but that is exactly the kind of excuse we offer when we do not behave in a Christian manner.

If we are not sure what areas we need to work on we should ask God for wisdom so that we will know. **James 1:5** - *If any of you lack wisdom, let him ask of God, that giveth to all men liberally, and upbraideth not; and it shall be given him.*

Ask with faith. **James 1:6** - *But let him ask in faith, nothing wavering. For he that wavereth is like a wave of the sea driven with the wind and tossed.*

As always, look to the Bible for everything – including how to live. There are all kinds of guidelines. Here are just a couple: Ephesians 4:22 – 32; Colossians 3: 5 – 10. As we read through these it is easy to find things that the guy sitting next to you is doing wrong. We are looking for areas of our own lives that we need to change.

One reason that we have so much trouble changing is because we have the attitude that we should just sit back and let the Holy Spirit do all of the work. We believe there should be some miraculous transformation requiring no work at all on our part.

When we are trying to change we need to look at our shortcomings – not someone else's. **Romans 14:10** - *But why dost thou judge thy brother? or why dost thou set at nought thy brother? for we shall all stand before the judgment seat of Christ.*

Remember that God looks at us as individuals. <u>Every</u> Christian will face God in judgement someday. When we are in front of God, and we will be, giving an account of our lives, our feeble little excuses are gonna sound pretty weak. **Romans 14: 11** *For it is written, As I live, saith the Lord, every knee shall* *bow to me, and every tongue shall confess to God.* **12** *So then every one of us shall give account of himself to God.*

Pray (**1 Thessalonians 5:17**) *Pray without ceasing.* Without prayer we might as well not even bother trying to change. Without the wonderful gift of two-way communication that the Lord has given us, we have no chance of getting his help. Pray for change. Be sincere and pray in faith.

<u>True</u> repentance is a requirement for change to occur. Unless we are actually repentant, we will have no sincere desire to change. Some people believe that God is so much a God of love that He just wants them to be happy. They truly believe that God sits by patiently waiting until our mood is just right and we have a moment to dedicate to Him. In that brief moment He does what He can until the next time He senses we are in etc. It the mood to try to work on our lives. That is not the way it works! If we are not careful we find ourselves sinning and thinking, "It's OK – God will forgive me. I can just keep up my little cycle of sinning and asking forgiveness".

1 John 1:9 - *If we confess our sins, he is faithful and just to forgive us our sins, and to cleanse us from all unrighteousness.*

Acts 8:22 - 22. *Repent therefore of this thy wickedness, and pray God, if perhaps the thought of thine heart may be forgiven thee.*

1 John 1:9 - *If we confess our sins, he is faithful and just to forgive us our sins, and to cleanse us from all unrighteousness.*

We are told over and over in the New Testament that Jesus taught that repentance is a requirement for forgiveness. Repentance means confession and a feeling of authentic remorse. Authentic remorse does not mean that we know that we intend to keep on with our life's little secrets, knowing that all we have to do is to ask God to forgive us. The fact is, if we conduct our lives like that, we are not being forgiven.

> **NOTE**: Since this is an easy area to get in trouble over I want to make sure that I have expressed my idea very carefully. I am <u>not</u> saying that God does not continue to forgive sin, day in and day out. What I <u>am</u> saying is this: If my plan is to sin, and while I am sinning, think to myself, "no problem, when I am through I'll just ask God to forgive me, and then I'm set until I decide to commit this exact same sin tomorrow." If that is my attitude, I am fooling myself, and I am not being forgiven. If you disagree, please show me the scripture that tells us it is OK to lie to God. Show me the scripture that says He will accept my false statement that I am sorry for what I did, when I am not. Show me anywhere in the entire Bible where there is any indication that God has ever forgiven a person, or a people, when they expressed no remorse and when they did not ask for forgiveness.

What are the requirements of true repentance? True repentance does not mean that you are sorry you got caught or that you are sorry you have to feel guilty, or that you got hurt, or even that you hurt someone else. True, Godly repentance means you are repentant because you ruined your relationship with God. You are remorseful because your joy and your walk with Him have been violated.

True Godly repentance should not be confused with an emotional feeling that we get sometimes. Feeling really bad for a moment is not even close to being truly remorseful and sincerely seeking a way to stop. It does not mean that we go to church, kneel down at the alter, or bow our heads at our seats and cry tears, while we tell God the same thing year in and year out; Then we leave and start the whole thing over again.

So – the first requirement for changing our lives – is true, grieving repentance. Remember this – it's not easy. But with God – it is very achievable

2 Corinthians 7:10 - *For godly sorrow worketh repentance to salvation not to be repented of: but the sorrow of the world worketh death.*

When we obtain true repentance we'll soon find that things that used to look good to us, now repulse us. Every person who was saved as an adult has looked back on their life and wondered how they could have enjoyed things that disgust them now. And the growth is on going. The longer we attempt to walk the Christian walk, the more we will succeed. This is not an implication that we will succeed while we are on earth, but we will do better every day. If you are a new Christian, I encourage you to verify this with folks who have been saved for awhile.

2 Timothy 2: 25 - *In meekness instructing those that oppose themselves; if God peradventure will give them repentance to the acknowledging of the truth;*

26 *And that they may recover themselves out of the snare of the devil, who are taken captive by him at his will.*

The devil is smart – how can I tell if I've really repented?

Psalms 51:16 - *For thou desirest not sacrifice; else would I give it: thou delightest not in burnt offering.* **17** *The sacrifices of God are a broken spirit: a broken and a contrite heart, O God, thou wilt not despise.*

In these verses David was repenting of his adultery. He was deeply broken, truly repentant, and <u>totally forgiven</u> by God. The Lord restored David's joy and performed many great things in his life. None of this would have happened without David's passionate plea for forgiveness and his expression of true sorrow.

Are we producing the kind of fruit that indicates true

repentance in our life. **Luke 3:8** - *Bring forth therefore fruits worthy of repentance, and begin not to say within yourselves, We have Abraham to our father: for I say unto you, That God is able of these stones to raise up children unto Abraham.* In other words, are we walking the talk that we talk to God when we ask forgiveness? And if not, why not? If your answer to this question is, "it's just too hard, I can't do it" you might be surprised to find out that I completely agree with you. The reason I agree is that I can't do it either. That is the entire point of this chapter. God can do it – and He is going to – if we want Him to. What are some of the fruits of true repentance?

No more excuses – When you are sincere you won't make excuses for failure. You'll quit blaming your job, your spouse, and your parents. You'll stop finding a million reasons why you should be the one exception to the prohibition against sin, because your circumstances are unique. We've already discussed the fact that we'll all face God. I'd hate to think that my plans was to explain to Him that it was not my fault I lived a life of unrepentant sin, I had just had a harder life than those who attempted to live right.

True Sorrow – No one can know if our sorrow for our sins is genuine. Sometimes we don't even know. Some people cry. Some people don't. Some need to kneel at the alter – some don't. The key is, do you feel the same anguish that David felt? Do you feel that anguish because you have lost the joy of your walk with God?

Confession of sin – We need to quit trying to fool ourselves – we are definitely not fooling God. If we're sincere we should level with God and confess our sins.

Fruits – Can the folks who are watching us tell a difference in our lives based upon the type of fruit we produce?

Take a look at **Romans 6: 1-7** Paul is telling us not to attempt to abuse the grace that God has shown us.

The moment Abraham Lincoln signed the emancipation proclamation all of the slaves in the United States were immediately free. History tells us that for various reasons some of them chose to stay with their former masters. Even though they were liberated, they allowed their former masters to control them. I'm sure all of them felt like they had sufficient reason for this.

The moment we are saved we are free from the hold that our former master, Satan, had on us. The problem is, some folks choose to allow him to maintain his former role as their master. And just like the slaves, we all have reasons we feel are valid. We don't have to sin. We choose to. Before Christ we had no choice – now we do. If a person is committing the same exact sin over and over and over – it is because they choose to. There is no power that any particular sin has to enslave us. That power has been broken by the sacrifice Jesus made for us. God expects us to exercise that power.

BOTTOM LINE

The next time we are tempted with the same old sin that we always fall prey to, we should remember what we've talked about. Think this, "God is watching me. I have no excuse. God knows that I know I am about to sin and that I am choosing to sin. If I choose to do this I am thumbing my nose at God – while He is watching. And I am doing it well aware that I'm doing wrong. **BUT** – I'm not gonna do this. This sin has **NO** power over me. I am dead to the power sin had over my life. I choose to follow the path God wants me to follow".

After you think that thought – don't go ahead and commit the particular sin and then run to God and ask for forgiveness … At least not if you plan to continue this little cycle. You are not fulfilling the spiritual requirements for true repentance.